LESSONS IN PROJECT MANAGEMENT

Tom Mochal and Jeff Mochal

Apress®

Lessons in Project Management

Copyright © 2011 by Tom Mochal and Jeff Mochal

ISBN-13 (pbk): 978-1-4302-3834-8
ISBN-13 (electronic): 978-1-4302-3835-5

Trademarked names may appear in this book. Rather than use a trademark symbol with every occurrence of a trademarked name, we use the names only in an editorial fashion and to the benefit of the trademark owner, with no intention of infringement of the trademark.

President and Publisher: Paul Manning
Lead Editor: Jeffrey Pepper
Editorial Board: Steve Anglin, Mark Beckner, Ewan Buckingham, Gary Cornell, Jonathan Gennick, Jonathan Hassell, Michelle Lowman, James Markham, Matthew Moodie, Jeff Olson, Jeffrey Pepper, Frank Pohlmann, Douglas Pundick, Ben Renow-Clarke, Dominic Shakeshaft, Matt Wade, Tom Welsh
Coordinating Editor: Jennifer L. Blackwell
Copy Editor: Mary Behr
Compositor: Mary Sudul
Indexer: SPi Global
Cover Designer: Anna Ishschenko

Distributed to the book trade worldwide by Springer-Verlag New York, Inc., 233 Spring Street, 6th Floor, New York, NY 10013. Phone 1-800-SPRINGER, fax 201-348-4505, e-mail orders-ny@springer-sbm.com, or visit www.springeronline.com.

For information on translations, please contact us by e-mail at info@apress.com, or visit www.apress.com.

Apress and friends of ED books may be purchased in bulk for academic, corporate, or promotional use. eBook versions and licenses are also available for most titles. For more information, reference our Special Bulk Sales–eBook Licensing web page at www.apress.com/bulk-sales.

My work on this book is dedicated to my wife Pam and my (now grown) children Lindsay, Sean, and Ashley. Without their love, support, and good humor, none of my work would be possible.
—Tom Mochal

For my wife Erika and our two amazing kids Emelia and Samuel. Thank you so much for your constant support and unconditional love. Special thanks to my brother and co-author, Tom, for allowing me to help tell these great stories and lessons on project management.
—Jeff Mochal

Contents

About the Authors

Tom Mochal, PgMP, PMP, TSPM is the President of TenStep (www.TenStep.com), a management consulting and training company with over 50 offices around the world. Tom is also the author of 10 additional books on a variety of project management, people management, and related topics. Tom is an internationally recognized speaker, lecturer, instructor, and consultant to companies and organizations around the world. He won the Distinguished Contribution Award from the Project Management Institute for his work spreading knowledge of project management around the world.

Jeff Mochal is currently Director, Communication and External Relations for ConAgra Foods, a Fortune 500 food company with net sales of $12.7 billion. Jeff is responsible for external communication for ConAgra Foods, developing and executing key media relations strategies designed to strengthen the reputation of ConAgra Foods and its brands with key stakeholder groups. Jeff has extensive expertise in crisis communication, issues management, change management, employee engagement, and media relations. He currently lives outside of Chicago and is pursuing his MBA from the University of Notre Dame.

Introduction

This book represents insights and experience gained from 30 years of experience working on projects, managing projects, and managing people who were managing projects. Like most project managers, I didn't learn formal project management before I started managing projects. Initially, managing projects just meant determining the work that needed to be done and working with one or more people to get it done. After managing projects a few times, I became more comfortable planning out the work and managing it to completion. These projects ranged from small and large enhancement projects to multimillion dollar initiatives.

This type of project management experience is typical of the way most people learn to manage projects. Most project managers have very little formal project management training and no mentoring at all. They do, however, have good organizational skills and a good feel for the work needed to complete the deliverables required for the project. If they are really good, they also have decent estimating skills, which will ensure they have enough budget and time to complete the project.

That was my story until the mid-1990s, when I was a director at a large beverage company. When I took the position, I inherited a number of projects—one of which was politically sensitive and under pressure to finish within a six-month deadline. The approach of the previous project manager seemed reasonable enough; however, it became clear the work involved with the project has been greatly underestimated. For a variety of reasons, the project took almost 18 months to go live—not the six months originally estimated.

The most frustrating part of this project for me was not being able to provide the guidance and coaching needed for the project manager. I didn't have the formal project management knowledge required to rescue it. At one point, I even set up daily meetings with the project manager, but it seemed a case of the blind leading the blind.

My next assignment at the same company was to build a Project Management Office (PMO) and deploy formal project management processes throughout the worldwide IT organization. I started as the contributor on this project and gradually acquired more responsibility until I became the program manager of the entire initiative. This allowed me to make the transition from the typical "seat-of-your-pants" project manager to one who understood the methodology side as well. When your job is to build the methodology and coach and train others, you gain an in-depth understanding of project management and how to do it well. So, that is what I did for three years.

After three years, I decided to leave the large company and I thought a lot about what I had learned. I spent most of my career managing work without formal project management training. Now I had formal training and experience using a large scale mega methodology. I wanted to apply my background and experience to create a project management process that project managers would understand and accept. The result is the TenStep® Project Management Process (TenStep) available at www.tenstep.com.

When I developed the TenStep Process, I focused on two overriding principles. First, the methodology would be scalable, meaning it would be easy to understand and apply for project managers managing small, medium, and large projects. This allows project managers to manage small projects with a minimum level of project management structure and not feel guilty. It also applies a much higher level of project management structure to large projects without apology.

Second, the 10 steps of the TenStep methodology would be aligned in a way that represents a progression of project management competencies. The lower steps represent processes every project manager should practice on every project. As the steps get higher, more rigor and sophistication are typically required, especially for larger and more complex efforts.

When I worked in the large PMO, I also had the pleasure of coaching and training project managers around the world. As I was doing this coaching, I realized it was easier for project managers to learn if I included examples within the lessons. For instance, it was easier for project managers to learn change management if I could apply the principle to their projects, including specific examples of applying scope change management plus instances of misusing the process. If I couldn't think of examples relevant to specific projects, I would come up with examples from other projects to which they could relate.

This book is the culmination of that teaching method. The marketplace is full of project management books, columns, best practices, tips, and traps. The question is not "Can you find project management techniques?" The question is "Will you remember the right techniques at the appropriate time to apply it on your project?"

Let's face it: very few columns or books are compelling enough to be read over and over again. That is the case with project management content. Project management books tend to get read once (or maybe just scanned) and never picked up again. I felt I could communicate a project management lesson more effectively if I could tell a story, a parable perhaps, that showcases a project management lesson. The reader would have the context of how the lesson really applies on a project. The lesson would then be easier to understand and, more importantly, to remember.

This book applies 50 important project management lessons in 50 easy-to-digest stories. In addition to the main lesson, each story also mixes in other project management concepts and definitions. I hope you find the information in this book valuable in your job, and I hope you can apply the lessons to your projects.

—Tom Mochal

The Year Begins—

On a Slippery Note

The snow was still falling, although lightly and with fewer flakes, as I stared out the bedroom window on the morning of January 4. I could already smell the coffee brewing downstairs in the kitchen, and I longed to pour myself a cupful to warm my insides. But last night's snowstorm had made a mess of the driveway, and I knew the only way my family and I were getting out of the house today was to start digging now. The storm had deposited about six inches of heavy snow, and it took about an hour to carve a clear path from the garage to the street. Time to invest in a snow blower, I thought.

The morning shovelling took much longer than anticipated, leaving me barely enough time to grab a shower and get dressed, let alone have breakfast with my now-awake wife, Pam, and our 5-year-old son, Tim. Sensing my anxiety and realizing I was running late, Pam poured my coffee and cream into a cup-sized Thermos and wrapped a couple pieces of toast in a paper towel. I grabbed both items, planted kisses on Pam and Tim, and headed out the garage door to start my day.

I had barely driven a block when I felt the back end of my Honda turn to the left, against my wishes, and begin skidding toward the curb. As I came to a stop, I could see in my rear-view mirror that the newly fallen flakes were hiding patches of ice underneath. The day had just begun and I had driven less than a half-mile from my house, but I knew one thing for certain—I was going to be late for my first day as Project Management Advisor at Mega Manufacturing.

Mega Manufacturing is the nation's fifth largest manufacturer. Like all large companies, they have a lot of projects and they want to improve how they manage these projects. The perception is that projects take too long, cost too much, and don't fully meet the company expectations.

One way to implement project management processes in a large organization is through a focused Project Management Office (PMO). Mega Manufacturing realizes this. Our company President wanted to start a major initiative this year to build a PMO and then use the PMO to build a better environment for project success. The plan was to start building a PMO in the IT organization and then elevate that organization to be an Enterprise PMO. However, budget tightening and a number of other business priorities forced this broader initiative to be postponed for a year.

I have been working at Mega for ten years and was recently assigned to a new position as Project Management Advisor. My position was funded as a temporary measure to start to prepare project managers for this larger initiative. It was a good opportunity for me, and I was excited to use my knowledge of project management to help others in the company become more efficient and successful with their projects. When I took the job, I knew I would have an opportunity to work with many project managers—some well trained and highly experienced, and some brand new to the concept. Jerry Ackerman was in the latter group. I was meeting him first thing that morning. I hoped that meeting went better than my morning commute.

Understand the Characteristics of a Project

Jerry and I had scheduled a meeting prior to the company closing for New Year's Day, and I found him waiting outside my office when I arrived.

"Jerry, I am terribly sorry to be so la—"

"Tom! Good to see you," he interrupted. "Don't be silly about being late. I just got here 15 minutes ago myself."

"It took me longer than anticipated to get the snow shovelled this morning. I must be moving slower in my old age!"

"A shovel? We need to get you a snow blower!"

I smiled at his suggestion, recalling I had similar thoughts just a few hours earlier.

Jerry and his wife, Barbara, were trying to buy their first house, but the hunt for the perfect home had been long and difficult. He shared some of those struggles with me, and we talked at great length about the house my wife and I purchased a few years ago.

"The right house will come along, Jerry. Did you see any you liked this weekend?"

"Not really, Tom. We looked at a few open houses on Sunday, but the weather prevented us from looking at any more. We are trying to remain optimistic, but it's really starting to drive us crazy."

"Well, stick with it," I said, trying to sound reassuring.

Jerry was a relatively new employee who worked in the Information Infrastructure department. He had big, blue eyes and a thick head of hair with shaggy sideburns. The sideburns and bushy hair gave him the slightly nerdish appearance that many people have come to expect of people who work with computers. If it was possible to tell such things based on a person's appearance, he also looked like someone who liked to work with technology more than people. He had just been given the responsibility of upgrading the company's phone system but wasn't sure he was ready for the task. The work involved inspecting the phone lines, replacing the lines where needed, and upgrading the software. Jerry predicted the effort would take four months to complete and cost upwards of $350,000. There would be six people involved, although not all full time.

After talking awhile longer about his house-hunting experiences, I asked Jerry if he wanted to talk a bit about his upcoming project.

"Sure," he said. "Actually, I am not sure there is anything you can help me with. Aren't you supposed to help project managers?"

I was initially taken aback, thinking I had perhaps missed something. "Well, yes. But it sounds like you have a pretty important project. Are you an experienced project manager?"

"Project? Project manager?" Jerry questioned, sounding unsure. "We don't do projects in this department. We just go ahead and get the work done."

The light bulb went off in my head, and I knew I was going to have my hands full. Not only was Jerry an inexperienced project manager, he didn't even know he was the project manager!

"Jerry," I said, "let's talk."

LESSON

Most work typically falls into one of the following categories:

- **Support work** is associated with keeping current production processes working and stable, such as fixing a crashed computer application.
- **Operations work** is associated with the ongoing execution of a company's business processes, such as entering accounting transactions or ordering supplies.
- **Overhead** includes vacation and sick time.
- **Management and leadership** is associated with the time spent managing people and moving the organization forward to achieve its business goals.
- **Projects** are temporary work used to do new things and build new or enhanced products.

Project work is the area of interest in my new job. Projects are not something only certain departments do—they are how work gets done. In fact, projects can exist in any functional area. This is a key difference between the work a person does and the organization where that person works. For instance, your department may execute some projects as well as perform support type work. Your operations area may execute projects as well as operations work. Your management team may even do projects in addition to their management work. This highlights the difference between your functional group and the actual type of work you perform. Although there are differing definitions of projects, all projects have three major characteristics—a finite time frame, uniqueness, and deliverables.

First and foremost, a project must have a start and end date. Although one could quibble about the exact dates, there must be a time before the work existed and there must be a time when the work no longer exists. Entering transactions into an accounting system, for instance, is not a project because the activity goes on indefinitely. Answering questions from the users about the accounting system software is not a project either, since those questions will be asked indefinitely as well. On the other hand, Jerry's work to upgrade the phone system was not happening before, and at some point it will be completed (even if it goes over its deadline, it will either be completed or cancelled). The phone system may be upgraded again, but if that happens, there will be a time gap between the upgrades, so the work is not continuous. The next upgrade will have a start and end date as well.

All projects are also unique. They have unique characteristics, unique deliverables, unique people, and unique circumstances. As a contrast, if you worked for the help desk, over time you would begin to master your job since there is a certain rhythm and pattern to the work. Once you get some experience, you find you can handle the repetitive nature of the work by following a certain set of processes and procedures. This is an example of ongoing operations. Working at the help desk today is similar to working there yesterday and it will be similar tomorrow and a year from tomorrow.

On the other hand, projects are unique. This characteristic makes them hard to estimate and hard to manage. Even if the project is similar to one you have done before, new events and circumstances will occur. Each project typically holds its own challenges and opportunities.

Lastly, all projects produce one or more deliverables (deliverables also may be called *products*). These deliverables could be anything from a computer application to an analysis document; from a recommendation to a new house. If the work does not result in the creation of one or more deliverables, then it is not a project. Even if your project is building a service, you would have deliverables such as a procedures manual, training classes, and perhaps marketing literature.

Most people also assign other characteristics to projects. These include a defined scope, a defined set of resources (people, money, equipment, supplies, etc.), common objectives (stated or unstated), and an assigned project manager and project team.

It is important to note there are no upper or lower limits in terms of effort, cost, or duration. A project might take 10,000 hours to complete, or it might take 10 hours to complete. Very small projects are typically called *enhancements* or *discretionary requests*. Of course, how one manages these small and large projects is not the same. The 10 hour project probably does not have any formal project management techniques applied to it at all. A large project will require much more rigor and structure.

Projects can be found in all types of businesses—from marketing to manufacturing to movie studios. Yes, even in the Information Infrastructure department where Jerry works! How many times have major initiatives failed because they were not organized and managed as a project? Many, many times. Jerry wants to just "get the work done." That type of thinking is fine for a 40-hour project where work can be planned and defined in your head. However, this initiative is too big, too complex, and too important for Jerry to manage in his head. He will have a better chance of success if he defines, structures, and manages the work as a project. When I meet with him next, the education process will continue.

Always Have an Identified and Committed Sponsor

The next day I had an opportunity to meet with Ashley Parker, the project manager on a large Marketing information database project that was just beginning a major new phase. Ashley was married and had two children. She often volunteered at her kids' school and helped out once a month at their neighborhood church. She was wearing dark pants with a plain red turtleneck and red-framed glasses when she came into my office at a little past 2 p.m. Good, solid business clothes—nothing fancy, but nothing odd either. On second look, the red glasses did give her a bit of pizzazz. Her hair was shoulder length, and she stood about 5' 3", even with heels on. She had a solid image, but I'd soon see if she was a solid project manager. I had known Ashley for about three years, although we had never really worked together before.

"Hello Ashley. How are you?" I asked as she entered my office.

"I am doing okay, I guess. Am I interrupting you?"

"Not at all. I'm just filling out a form for new business cards."

Ashley smiled and sat down in the chair in front of my desk. She had a look of concern on her face, so I asked her to give me an update on her project. She informed me that her team had just completed phase one of the project. The next phase needed to start right away, but she wasn't sure the business client was fully involved. The original business sponsor had recently been reassigned, and Ashley hadn't met the new manager in that role.

We discussed her situation for a few minutes.

"In today's rapidly changing business environment, it is not uncommon for companies to experience turnover of key project resources," I explained. "The Marketing and Sales department seems to have more people coming and going than most. That's one reason it makes sense to break large projects down into phases, each of which can be managed as an individual project. You are very smart to use this approach. Whenever you complete one phase, you always have a chance for a checkpoint to make sure everything is ready to proceed to the next phase."

"Thanks," she responded.

"Did you complete a Project Charter document before the project started?" I asked.

"Yes, I did," she answered.

"How old is it?"

"It was written and approved four months ago."

"I assume your previous sponsor approved the project. Has the new sponsor seen the Project Charter?"

"I don't think so," Ashley responded. "He has so many things on his mind; I don't think our project is on his radar screen yet."

"You are entering a new phase," I confirmed with Ashley, who nodded. "Have you updated the Project Charter to reflect the new work?"

Ashley shook her head. "We haven't been able to get the time we need from the sponsor and the client to validate the remaining work."

"Okay, the worst thing would be to continue the project without business involvement and then have to redo much of the work later on—or even cancel the whole project for lack of sponsorship. Let's not keep things going based on their own momentum. Now is the time to revalidate business commitment and sponsorship, and make sure you are still on the right track. Then you can refocus the team for the next phase."

LESSON

The term *client* is used in multiple contexts. Sometimes the term refers to a specific person and sometimes the term refers to the group of people receiving the project benefit. For instance, if you say, "The client asked us to include some new requirements," you may be referring to a specific person or you may be referring to the generic client organization. Some organizations use the term *customer* or *user* to refer to the person or group receiving value from the project. At Mega Manufacturing, we use the term *client*.

Sponsors have ultimate authority over projects, and they are almost always within the client organization. In most companies, the simplest way to identify the sponsor is to ask who is providing funding for the work. The sponsor also resolves major issues and changes, approves major deliverables, and provides high-level direction. The sponsor acts as a champion for the project within his or her organization—and elsewhere as needed. If the project is large and the sponsor is senior enough in the company, he or she may take on the role of executive sponsor and delegate the day-to-day decision making to a lower-level project sponsor.

Typically, a project would not get funded or started without a sponsor. However, in some projects, the sponsor tends to sink into the background and does not remain actively engaged in the project. When this happens, the client organization can start to lose interest and focus. Good project managers should make sure this never happens. The sponsor should be kept as actively involved as possible. To accomplish this, project managers should meet with the sponsor regularly, keep him or her informed of project progress, and frequently ask for direction and advice.

All projects need an active sponsor—either an executive sponsor or a tactical project sponsor. If the project does not have an active sponsor, the project manager may feel obligated to fill the void and make many of the business decisions that are really the responsibility of the sponsor. This may keep the project going in the short term but almost always results in a less than optimal solution from a business perspective.

Unfortunately, even an engaged sponsor sometimes leaves in the middle of a project. This is the situation Ashley faces. She has a project in progress and is ready to move from one phase to the next. Many project managers would be tempted to just keep the project moving and continue working until someone tells them to stop. Ashley, however, recognizes that this is not right because two very big problems can occur.

First, new sponsors have new ideas and new requirements. To a certain extent, that is the privilege of being the sponsor. Ashley wants to make sure she understands any differences between the desires of the old sponsor and the new one. Otherwise, she may end up having to perform more work later when the new sponsor finally has more time to pay closer attention.

Second, transitioning from one sponsor to another can lead to a lack of focus from the client organization. Ashley recognizes this since she told me her clients were not as engaged as they should be. This usually manifests itself in the form of unanswered phone calls, unreturned messages, missed meetings, or missed deadlines. In Ashley's case, the loss of focus from her client organization is probably directly related to the loss of her original sponsor.

It's not easy to stop a project, especially since the resources allocated to the project could become idle or could potentially be reassigned. However, Ashley cannot continue without an identified sponsor and client commitment. She should talk to her manager and the client manager about validating who the new sponsor will be and get him or her engaged soon. If the project is still important to the client, Ashley should be able to get a new sponsor involved, reenergize the client group, and continue the work. If she cannot get a new client sponsor, she and her manager need to put the project on hold. It would be a potentially painful step, but not as painful to the company as completing an irrelevant project. Once clients understand that a project will be put on hold, they will have to make a decision on its relevant importance. If it is important enough, it will receive the proper level of focus. If not, the project will probably not be continued.

Report Status on All Projects

Mega Manufacturing is headquartered in Dickens, Illinois, population 90,000. The laid-back town is located about 55 miles northeast of Chicago, and Mega Manufacturing is by far its leading industry. The second biggest source of jobs in the town is Northeast Illinois State University, a small liberal arts college with an annual student population of 8,000. Pam and I moved to Dickens 11 years ago when I was hired in Mega's IT department. Several months after we moved, the university hired Pam as ticket coordinator in the Athletics department. She is currently sports information director for the university, a title she has held for the last three years.

Although fairly small, the town is genuinely charming and very beautiful, with many tree-lined streets and an open, inviting attitude. We tell our out-of-town friends our city is very family friendly, with great schools, plenty of parks, and a low crime rate. And when we want to get away for the weekend, we just hop in the car and head for Chicago.

That's exactly what Mike Miller did over the weekend. He and his family spent Saturday and Sunday in Chicago, catching a Bulls game on Saturday night. Mike was a popular employee in our office and had a great

great reputation as a patient, thoughtful man who would bend over backwards to help a friend or colleague. His office was full of family photos, including several pictures of his kids in their baseball uniforms, soccer uniforms, and his youngest daughter in a ballerina tutu. He asked me to stop by on January 13 to discuss a project he was doing to install document management software in the Legal department.

"How is life treating you Mike?" I asked as I entered his office.

"Oh, good and bad, Tom," he responded. "The kids and I just got back from a fun weekend in Chicago catching the Bulls crush the Cleveland Cavaliers. So that was good."

"And what's the bad?"

"Well, it's this darn project I am working on. That's why I asked you to stop by today. I could really use your advice, Coach."

I smiled. Mike gave me the nickname "Coach" at last year's annual New Year's Eve party when my transfer was announced. He liked to call people by nicknames, and I had to admit the practice carried a certain degree of charm and camaraderie. Mike always made you feel like a friend, even if you were meeting him for the first time.

"Give me some of the details, Mike. What exactly is the problem?"

"My sponsor saw a report on the desk of the finance director showing the status on a big project underway in the finance area. He started to ask questions, and now it turns out I need to do a status report as well."

"Interesting," I said. "Sounds like you don't currently report status. Is that right?"

"No, we don't," Mike said. "Now my sponsor wants a status report like the one from finance. This report is four pages long and contains more detail than we track here. It's going to take us a long time to get the report done—time we could be spending working on the project."

I could see where this was leading. "Don't you consider communicating with your business clients part of your work on the project?" I asked.

"We were communicating fine without having to do a four-page status report. We always took time to let the client know what was going on whenever he asked. You know, it's all this paperwork that turns people against methodology."

"Project managers need to consider effective, proactive communication as part of their job," I replied. "But let's be clear: there is a difference between 'reporting status' and 'status reports.'"

LESSON

Many years ago, a good project manager might have gotten away with being a poor communicator. The clients typically didn't like it, but as long as project managers could deliver the goods, clients were inclined to let them do their own thing.

In today's world, however, projects need to be undertaken in partnership with clients, and the partnership absolutely requires solid communication. If you are managing a large project, you may have a multifaceted communication approach. On a smaller project, the communication needs are simpler. However, reporting status is not an option. It is a requirement on all projects, large and small.

Status reporting can take many forms depending on the size of the project. The project manager may request that team members submit status reports on a weekly, biweekly, or monthly basis. These reports are used by the project manager to understand the detailed status of the work against expected target dates. These team status reports also include specific problems, concerns, and risks that team members are encountering.

The project manager also creates status updates for his or her functional manager, as well as the sponsor and other stakeholders. This status report contains summarized information that is of more interest to these stakeholders. These are typically written documents, although they could be e-mail messages or web page updates. They could even be voicemail messages.

In addition to status reports, most projects have some form of status meeting. Again, these could be at different levels. The project manager might have a weekly status meeting with members of the team and a separate status meeting with sponsors, managers, and a steering committee. Typically one meeting will not suffice, since the level of detail and audience interest is vastly different between senior management and the project team.

The main function of status reporting is to communicate project accomplishments, but you should also use it to highlight any major problems, changes, risks, etc. The purpose of status reporting is to manage expectations and to ensure that all participants and stakeholders have a common understanding of the project today and what the future looks like. No one likes surprises. Proactive and ongoing communication is the key to making it all work.

It sounds like Mike does not see proactive communication as a core responsibility of the project manager. Mike is a reactive communicator. He says he provides a full status of the project whenever his sponsor asks for it, but what he doesn't realize is this lack of effective, proactive communication is exactly what is causing the sponsor to request additional information in the form of a formal status report.

My discussion with Mike centers around two main points.

- Proactive communication is absolutely part of the job of a project manager. The ability to proactively anticipate the communication needs of your stakeholders is one of the criteria separating casual project managers from mature and professional project managers.
- *Reporting status* is not the same as a *status report*. Reporting status is something all project managers need to do. Paper status reports are just one delivery mechanism.

While the sponsor has requested a specific four-page status report he saw elsewhere, there are probably many alternatives. Mike should talk with the sponsor to determine what his information needs are, and then provide that information. Managers do not want to see the day-to-day minutia that is occurring on the project. They usually want you to stick to the major facts and tell them if they should be worried about anything. A common technique is to report the status of a project with an overall color code of green (okay), yellow (caution), or red (in trouble). Remember as well that the status report is a recap. If any major problems or events occur during the month, you should be communicating at the time of the occurrence.

It sounds like Mike's department does not have a standard status reporting process, so he'll need to work with the sponsor on how to best meet the sponsor's desire for more project information. Generally, the sponsor will be reasonable. If certain types of information are hard to report, chances are he will not require it. As mentioned earlier, there are many ways to report status. A formal status report document may not be needed at all.

Understanding the informational needs of your stakeholders is a part of communications planning. This should be done at the beginning of a project. Mike is playing catch-up now, but this experience should strengthen his understanding of this critical project management function so he can do better in the future.

Focus on Deadline Dates

January 15 brought an unusual amount of excitement and happiness to the office, especially considering we had just been hit with our second big snowstorm of the year. I figure the joyful spirit was attributable to it being payday. I heard a lot of people talking about overspending during the holidays and how they were in need of a financial shot in the arm. I, too, spent more than I planned and was excited to get my first paycheck as project management advisor. My promotion came with a nice raise, but I wasn't sure what my new semi-monthly compensation would be after taxes. I received my paycheck by mid-morning and was pleased with the new total.

Leaning back in my office chair, I picked up the framed picture on my desk of Tim as a newborn baby and stared in amazement at how little he was at birth and how quickly he was growing. He had bright green eyes like his mother and a big head like his dear old dad. I was still staring at his picture when Lindsay Peterson arrived. Her quiet knock broke my trance, and I stood up quickly to greet her.

"Lindsay, come in, come in! Sorry I didn't see you right away."

"That's okay, Tom," she replied. "I find myself doing the same thing with my new girl."

Lindsay worked in the Application Support area and had recently returned from maternity leave after the birth of her daughter Patricia in November. Her husband Al was a carpenter by trade and made quite a lot of money as an insurance contractor. I had not seen Lindsay in several months, but she looked much the same, with the addition of black circles under her eyes. As a parent, I understood about sleepless nights with a newborn.

"So how is life with little Patricia?"

"You know, she is only two months old, but I already find it hard to remember life without her. She is such a wonderful little baby, and she brings so much joy to Al and me. We'll have to invite you and Pam over for dinner one night so you can see her."

I thanked her for the offer and took a few minutes to peruse the pictures of Patricia she pulled from her purse. She was a cute baby with a round face and blue eyes. I was a little surprised to see she was bald, though, as Lindsay and Al both had full, thick heads of hair.

"So please tell me about your project," I said, returning to my chair.

Lindsay's Application Support team did not do projects often, but when they did, the projects tended to be complex. Her current project was a good example. She was managing a complex enhancement to a Sales department application. They had the most knowledge of this package, since they supported it on an ongoing basis.

"I'm not sure what to do," she began. "I've got good people on the team, but we are falling behind schedule. Some team members have been unable to allocate the time required to get the work done on schedule. Most of them are trying to balance work on my project with their other support responsibilities. When the current release has problems, they need to shift time over for that."

"How are you managing the project plan and keeping track of end dates?" I inquired.

"Every Wednesday and Friday I ask the team to give me an update. I ask for the number of hours spent on each assigned activity and what percent is complete. The problem is it seems that the work is always 90 *percent complete. By the time it's 100 percent complete, we have missed the deadline. When I talk to people about the project falling behind, they tell me they haven't been able to allocate the time the activity requires. If the activity takes 40 hours of effort, they don't consider it a problem unless they go over 40 hours. If it takes them a week longer to work all 40 hours, they still think they are doing okay."*

I drilled a little deeper. "What is the purpose of asking people how many hours they worked on each activity?"

Lindsay was a little puzzled. "Having the team report hours tells me how much time they are spending on each project activity and helps me to validate how close the original estimates were."

"Okay. I think you are getting that information," I agreed. "But it's not enough. You're falling behind. What information would be the most helpful for future project planning?"

She thought for a minute. "The deadline dates are really the most important. What I really want to know is when the work will be done."

LESSON

Have you ever managed a project where the work was always 90 percent complete? After a period of frustration, you realize that asking people what percentage of work is complete is only of limited value.

Estimating effort hours is important in setting up the original schedule and determining completion dates. But once the schedule is created and activities are assigned, the focus should switch to getting the work done on time. This does not mean actual effort hours are unimportant. They are important—especially if you are charging a client on an hourly basis, or if the project team contains contract resources charged on an hourly basis.

However, in a typical internal project utilizing internal resources, it is easier and more effective to manage the project based on the assigned end dates. Then just one question needs to be asked and validated: When will the work be done?

Lindsay's project showcases a common scenario. An activity may have been estimated to take 40 effort hours and two weeks to complete. Of the two estimates, the more important aspect of success is whether the work was completed within the two weeks. To a certain extent, it really doesn't matter if the actual effort took 30 hours or 60—as long as it is completed within two weeks (assuming, of course, there are no charges for each excess hour of work). When Lindsay receives status updates from the team, she should validate whether each activity will be completed by its deadline. If team members think it will, then Lindsay is fine. If they don't think it will, then Lindsay can take corrective action if necessary.

Regardless of how diligent your team members are, some deadlines will still be missed. If the work is not complete, the project manager's question is still "When will the work be done?" This line of questioning eliminates the problem of an activity being 90 percent complete, then 95 percent complete, then 99 percent complete but one, two, and then three weeks late. Asking for the completion date also allows the team member to personally recommit to a new deadline date. This personal commitment makes the team member more motivated to actually meet the deadline date.

There are reasons for keeping track of percent complete at a project level for those using Earned Value Management techniques. There are also reasons to keep track of actual effort hours. However, for schedule management, focus on when the work will be done. Managing the effort hours and the budget are two indicators of success, but managing by completion date is the best way to keep a project focused on its deadlines.

Apply Some Level of Project Management Discipline

—Even On Small Projects

Susan Chang phoned me on January 19 and asked for a quick meeting the next day to discuss her manufacturing project. When I arrived at her office she was on the phone, although she motioned for me to come in. Susan had straight black hair which she often wore pulled back with a clip or rubber band. She was born in Taiwan, but her parents were killed when she was a baby. An American soldier adopted her and brought her back to the States to live with him and his wife in Dickens. She was now in her early 30s. My knowledge of her came mostly from other people, although I did chat with her briefly at the New Year's Eve party and she told me some of her background. Taking my seat, I can hear her saying "Mommy needs to go now, sweetie." After she hung up, she explained that her youngest was home sick from school.

"She wanted to tell me her grandma was going to make her grilled cheese and chicken soup for lunch. She just loves grilled cheese."

"That's funny," I said. "How long has she been sick?"

"Only a few days," she replied. "It's just a cold, but you know how quickly those germs can spread. We figured it would be in everyone's best interest to keep her home for a few days."

One of the things I did know about Susan was that she was a germ freak. She kept little moist towelettes in her desk drawer to wipe off the phone and doorknobs periodically, and she also washed her hands more than anyone else I knew.

"Probably best," I offered. "So tell me, Susan, what's going on with your project?"

"Well, our client is very upset with us right now," she began. "The client's request started off simply enough. First, we were asked to create a new report to show the manufacturing run rate over the previous three months. Then, as we were finishing this off, he decided he wanted us to estimate the run rates over the next three months as well."

"Did you note this as a change?" I asked.

"No," Susan replied quickly. "We don't do projects in our group—just small enhancements. The original request should have only taken us 20 hours to complete. That's the typical size of the enhancements we perform."

I thought for a second about her comment "We don't do projects in our group" and was reminded of my meeting with Jerry a few weeks back.

"That's fine for the initial request," I replied. "But how about the changes the client is asking for now?"

Susan hesitated for a few seconds. "That was a more complex piece of work requiring a few extra weeks. We didn't have all of the data we needed, so we had to make some changes to capture the right information. We also had some trouble understanding how the new report should be calculated."

I was starting to get the picture. "Okay, how much time has been spent on this?"

"It's hard to say," she answered. "But we've had one to two people assigned to this for the last six weeks."

Six weeks! No wonder the client is unhappy!

LESSON

This situation occurs all the time. You start off with a small request that seems easy to complete. Then, before you know it, you have spent weeks and hundreds of hours on it. How did you end up in such straits? You may have just misunderstood and underestimated the original request. But what's more likely is that the original, simple request has become more complicated thanks to additional changes, additions, and revisions from the client.

Earlier, when I defined a project, I said enhancements are considered projects because they have a beginning and an end, they result in a deliverable, and they have resources applied. An enhancement that takes 1,000 hours to complete is easy to categorize as a project. You can tell right away that it is big. However, Susan's small enhancement fits the definition of a project as well.

If this was a formal project, Susan would have developed a Project Charter that included a description of scope. Of course, Susan cannot be expected to manage a 20-hour request as a formal project. These types of projects can be planned and managed in her head. However, Susan did not recognize the fact that her request had evolved from a 20-hour project into one that will take hundreds of hours to complete. At this point, the work has already consumed several weeks and a couple hundred hours—and it is not over yet! Looking back, the work should have been run as a small- to medium-sized project.

How should you manage work that starts off small but ends up being much larger? The answer is to manage small requests informally but use the appropriate project management techniques when necessary. In Susan's case, when she received the major change, she should have performed some basic change management. If Susan did not understand the impact, she should have asked for time to further investigate. She could have then done a more complete analysis of the new work and created a new estimate of the effort hours and duration required to complete the changes. She would then have had more solid information to take back to the client to validate that he understood the impact of the changes in terms of time and effort.

If she had talked to the client and explained to him the consequences, he could have made a decision as to whether the incremental value of the request was worth the extra time and effort. This would have been a good use of informal change management.

When the work became larger, Susan should have also started communicating more proactively, creating weekly status updates to better manage the client's expectations. In many cases, it is not the time delay that the client is upset about; it is the lack of communication explaining the status and the challenges. Again, if the client was better informed as to the consequences of his request, he may have realized earlier that the request was not worth this level of effort.

It does not usually make sense to stop a small piece of work and go through a formal project planning stage when the work starts to grow. However, that assumes the change only requires an incremental increase in effort and time. For instance if a 40-hour project grows to be 60 hours, you don't need to go through formal change management or formal planning.

On the other hand, if the work ends up being more substantial than originally thought, other project management practices may come into play, including better defining the work, building a simple schedule, and formally managing scope, issues, and communication. This is the case with Susan's project. It started off small and she managed it informally. That's fine. However, she should have recognized when the subsequent project changes caused the scope and effort of the project to increase substantially; that was the time to introduce more formal project management discipline and techniques—including better project communications with the client.

Define and Plan the Work First

I had been looking forward to my second meeting with Jerry for several days. His office was in a separate wing of our building, and I rarely saw him during the day. In fact, I had only seen him in person once since our initial meeting and that was in the first-floor cafeteria when we were both grabbing a quick sandwich before afternoon meetings.

Jerry was still finding his way at Mega Manufacturing and was still a novice when it came to project management. We had been e-mailing each other a couple times a week for the last three weeks, and I was really beginning to feel like part of his team. Although I was not doing any of the work related to his upgrade of the phone mail system, I did feel like I was part of the planning process, advising Jerry on how best to get the job done. I had a personal stake in seeing Jerry and his project succeed because I felt that advising him was exactly why I was given the position as project management adviser.

Jerry and I had agreed to meet for lunch, and I was reading the morning paper when I saw him enter the lunchroom. I usually eat lunch at my desk unless I am meeting with someone, so relaxing and reading the paper seemed like a luxury.

"Hey, Jerry. Glad to see you again," I said as I shook his hand.

"Good to see you again, too, Tom. Thanks for all the help you've been providing. I really appreciate it."

"Not a problem. I am glad to be of help. How are you doing?"

"Well, I am beginning to feel a bit overwhelmed, to be honest with you. It's partly because of this project and partly because of our house frustrations."

"You guys still haven't found a house?"

"No. In fact, we have lost a little bit of our enthusiasm about it. My wife is busy at her job, too, so we have not been able to devote a lot of time and energy to it lately. Our realtor sends us daily updates with links to new houses on the market or price changes, and it's nice to be able to look at the pictures online, but nothing has really panned out."

"What sort of things are you looking for?"

"Well, Barbara would like to have an older home, something with some charm and character. But we both like some of the modern conveniences like central air and a newer kitchen. We would also like a big master bedroom, and we both seem to like more open and spacious floor plans. It's amazing how many homes in Dickens don't have central air conditioning. I guess it's hard to think about that now since it is so cold. But come the summer, it gets so hot and humid here."

"Well, it certainly sounds like you know exactly what you are looking for in a house. I guess the question is whether you can find what you want in this market. I am sure if you keep looking, you will find something."

Jerry and I began eating our lunches and talked a bit more about houses. In time, the conversation turned back to work, and we began discussing his phone mail project. I could tell he was struggling with the ideas behind project management and still wanted to focus his attention on "just getting the work done." Unfortunately, I had been hearing some complaints around the office about the initial progress of the team's work, and I thought it was important to address them right away.

"So, tell me, how are things progressing with your project?" I asked, putting down my turkey sandwich.

"Everything is going well. We have made some good progress."

"I'm sure you have," I replied. "But I heard there was some trouble when you tried to rewire the second floor. My understanding is that many people were disrupted because they lost phone access for two days."

"Yes, but it wasn't totally our fault," he protested quickly. "We didn't realize we had to do both sides of the floor. We thought that only half the phone lines needed to be rewired."

"You and I have been discussing the need for planning more before your team jumps in to begin working. Do you think more planning would have helped in this case?"

Jerry realized where my question was heading. His initial philosophy was all about "just doing the work." Now he was open to a better alternative.

LESSON

It is not uncommon at the completion of a project to look back and reflect on how the project progressed. This is called an End-of-Project Review Meeting. For projects that were challenged or unsuccessful, these meetings are sometimes called *postmortems*. When the team discusses the reason for problems, a common theme seems to dominate—a general lack of definition and planning. A common lament is, "We should have spent more time planning." Of course planning is a big topic. It means you should have spent more time understanding the nature of the work, expectations, deliverables, scope, estimates, risks, etc.

People ask how much time should be spent in the planning phase of a project. The answer is simple: you need to spend sufficient time planning to make sure you know what you are doing. All projects should start with an up-front definition and planning process. The planning process scales depending on the size of the project. If it's a small project, the process does not have to be elaborate. The planning may take place in your head. On the other hand, if it's a very large project, the planning process itself could take many months and thousands of hours. The time spent adequately planning the work will be more than made up for by a smoother running and more focused project over the long term.

The up-front planning work involves four major aspects.

- **Defining the work**: This is the process of defining objectives, scope, risks, assumptions, etc. This information needs to be documented by the project manager and approved by the project sponsor to ensure there is a common understanding of the nature of the project. Defining the work tells you "what" you are doing.
- **Building a project schedule**: The schedule tells you "how" you will execute the project. The schedule lists the activities, estimated length, estimated effort, resources applied, dependencies between the activities, etc. At any given time, the schedule reflects your best guess of the work required to complete the project.
- **Allocating a project budget**: The budget reflects the estimated cost of the project and how those costs will be allocated. The budget reflects the costs of all the resources required to complete the project (labor and non-labor). The budget may not be as important if you are using internal resources on the project and if you are not charging back for the hours.
- **Defining the Project Management Plan (if appropriate)**: The Project Management Plan describes the processes you will use to manage the project. This includes the processes you will use to manage risk, scope, communication, quality, procurement, etc. A formal Project Management Plan is generally not needed for a small project but is absolutely vital as projects get larger.

They say that in every failure there is an opportunity to learn. In general, I agree with this, but what I really wish is that we could get the learning without the failure. I feel this way about Jerry. I spoke to Jerry earlier about defining and planning his work, but he never really bought into the value until now. Before today, he was polite and tried to follow some of what I was suggesting, but I could tell his heart was not in it. He had not internalized the benefit of "sufficient" planning.

When we discussed the problem he encountered rewiring the second floor, Jerry suddenly realized that more planning and a better understanding of what was required for this portion of the project might have avoided the mistake. An investment of a few more hours of planning may have resulted in closer estimates, better resource allocation, and getting the work done right the first time. Now I sense Jerry will try harder to plan the remainder of the project, instead of just giving it lip service.

Don't "Microbuild" or Micromanage the Workplan

After my first month on the job, I felt like things were going very well. I had met with many people at Mega Manufacturing, and I felt my work was helping people to save valuable time, while also making the company money by increasing productivity. I was also further strengthening an old friendship with Wayne Moretti, a vice president and my new boss.

Wayne and I went back a long way. He hired me as an associate IT specialist right out of college, when we both lived and worked in New York, and took an interest in my professional growth and development. Later, after I had moved to Atlanta and Wayne had moved to Dickens, he convinced me to relocate back to the Midwest and join him at Mega

Manufacturing. After a long career, Wayne announced last December that he would be retiring this year at the age of 60.

It was Wayne who first talked to the CIO about staffing a position to help people manage projects. The IT department at Mega Manufacturing realized it needed to manage projects in a better way. The medium-term direction was to build a Project Management Office and utilize a common set of project management processes throughout the organization. However, budget cutbacks and competing priorities had pushed this back for at least one year. This year Wayne was able to gain approval for a project management advisor—me. After discussing the position with Wayne for a couple weeks, I decided to accept it. Wayne's backing gave me instant credibility in the office, and I found myself very busy quickly.

Before I stepped into this role, Wayne spent time mentoring project managers in his department, but he felt he was only moderately successful. He didn't feel he had the focused time or the right level of project management competency himself to be a strong mentor. One of the people Wayne worked with was Reyna Andersen. Reyna was a few months into a large project to implement the first phase of a basic customer relationship management (CRM) package at our company. Wayne wanted me to meet with her to begin offering counsel when needed.

"Why don't you tell me about your current situation?" I asked Reyna when we met in her office Monday morning. "Wayne told me you ran into a little glitch."

"Well, when I built the schedule, I added a 15 percent allocation for project management work," Reyna began. "But I find myself spending more time than that. The schedule administration is really adding up. I am assigning work, following up to make sure it is completed, and updating the schedule. But it seems that's all I ever do."

I asked Reyna if I could have a look at the schedule. She handed me a stack of paper almost too painful to hold. "Wow!" I exclaimed, as I thumbed through the schedule. "This thing weighs more than the Yellow Pages! You have more than 1,200 activities listed over the next four months!"

"Well, it is comprehensive," Reyna replied proudly. "I want to make sure I understand the work to be done, and that my team does as well."

"You do need to understand the work to be done," I agreed. "Your team members need to understand as well. But you are probably giving them *more direction than they need. For instance, I see an activity for setting up a biweekly meeting. Why do you have five subtasks for this activity?"*

Reyna gave me the detailed response. "Well, you have to determine the participants, perform a calendar search, get a conference room, schedule the free time, and notify everyone."

"You're right; those all are steps to setting up a meeting," I concluded. "But remember what you said about understanding the work to be done? Don't you think if you just had one activity for setting up the meeting, you and your team would still know what to do?"

LESSON

There is no hard-and-fast rule to describe the level of detail you should use to define activities in your schedule. However, there are two rules of thumb.

First, as Reyna suggested, the schedule must be at a level where both the project manager (Reyna) and the project team can understand the work. That is why the schedule may be at different levels of granularity for different activities. If a piece of work is well understood, it can be placed on the schedule at a higher level. However, if the nature of the assignment is not clear, then the activity should be broken down into its more basic components (in some companies, these lowest-level statements are called *tasks*). The project manager may even need to have a meeting with other team members to determine exactly what needs to be done for some larger activities.

The second rule of thumb is that the schedule must be at a level that allows you to control the work. In general, an activity should never be longer than two weeks of duration. This would translate to around an 80-hour activity if you assign it to one full-time person. If the person is half-time, perhaps the largest activity is 40 hours. On the other hand, if you assign work to a subteam of three full-time people, the activity might be up to 240 effort hours (two weeks of 40 hours each, times three people).

One of the key elements of schedule management is to understand that you do not really know the status of an activity while it is in progress. Yes, the team member may say they are 50 percent done or they may tell you they can still hit the deadline. But you don't really know for sure until the deadline date (or when the work is completed). This means if you assign an activity that is estimated to be completed in two weeks or less, you should never have to wait more than two weeks to understand whether the work is on track or not. If it is not completed, you have time to address any problems and take corrective action.

This two-week rule is a good rule of thumb if you are working on a typical six-month project. However, what if your project is two months long? In that case, the two-week rule may not be appropriate because you may not have enough time for corrective action once you determine an activity is late. For example, if you assign an activity with a deadline of three weeks, your project may be almost half over before you fully realize there is a problem. Since the project is so short, a better high end for an activity might be one week. Likewise, if you have a very short project of one month, perhaps no activity should be longer than three days. In fact, if you are in the last week of a project, you may be assigning short duration work that is no longer than a few hours. In all of these cases, if you have an activity that requires more effort or duration than your threshold, you need to break the larger activity into one or more smaller activities.

Reyna likes to control things, but she is not following the first rule of thumb: she is not leaving the schedule at a level where the project manager and team members understand the activities. Reyna has fallen into the trap of building the schedule at too discrete a level. This has caused it to become inflated, cumbersome, and very hard to manage. Adding ten activities to the schedule where five will suffice (or perhaps one) adds extra work from a planning perspective and from a management perspective. Updating the schedule takes much longer, and understanding the remaining work of the project is much more difficult. The worst part is the extra activity produces very little incremental value, and is, in fact, detrimental. Reyna does not need that level of detail to manage the work and her team does not need that level of detail to understand what is needed.

Reyna has allocated 15 percent of the project effort hours toward project management activities. This is a good rule of thumb and should be plenty of time. She needs to free up more of her time by simplifying the schedule dramatically. When she does, she will still be able to control the project, but she will free herself up from the reactive drudgery caused by micromanaging. As I mentioned earlier, there is a time for very close schedule management using very short duration activities. This happens at the end of a project, phase, or when you are dealing with problems. This is the time when micromanaging may be appropriate. But you don't normally need this level of schedule control and this is not the way that you would typically manage.

If you feel you are spending too much time managing the schedule and assigning work, you may be right. Make sure you are managing work at a level where you and your team members can understand the work assignments, while at the same time maintaining proactive control so that you can respond appropriately if problems arise.

Hire a Diverse Project Team

Without Compromising on the Best Candidates

On February 7, I asked Jerry to stop by my office to discuss the current status of his project to upgrade the phone mail system. I was also anxious to share with him the news regarding the Morettis' house going on the market. He was wearing a light brown sweater when he walked into my office, and it looked like he got a haircut recently. It was still shaggy, but not as shaggy as usual.

"Have a seat, Jerry. I have really been looking forward to meeting with you today."

"Why is that, Tom?" he asked with a puzzled look on his face.

"Tell me, have you guys had any luck finding a house?"

Jerry talked for five minutes on the continuing struggle he and his wife were having. They were only looking at houses every other weekend now and were fast growing weary of the hunt. I was trying hard to listen to his concerns, but finally I couldn't hold back any longer.

"Jerry, I might have found the perfect house for you guys!"

He could tell I was excited and asked me to tell him the story. I gave him all the information I could think of on Wayne's house, and I could see Jerry's expression growing brighter and brighter the more I talked. I agreed to meet him and his wife for lunch on Sunday and bring them by the Morettis' house so they could have a quick tour. He was so excited that he almost left my office to call his wife. I convinced him to stay a few minutes longer to brief me on the status of his project.

"So, how have things been going on your project? Did you put a good team together?" I asked.

"I think I did, Tom," Jerry replied. "I personally interviewed all of the candidates to make sure we got the best possible workers. In fact, a lot of the team members remind me a lot of myself! I think it's going to be easy working with a group like that. We are having a few minor problems in the early-going, though. I thought it would be a fairly simple task to gather requirements from the client, but it's not going so well. It's almost like they're from another planet!"

"What do you mean by that?" I asked. "I have managed a lot of projects and encountered a lot of problems, but working with aliens has never been one of them!"

"Well," Jerry started, "I recall managing similar projects in the past and I assumed that this client would have similar expectations as previous ones. But a lot of their needs are completely foreign to me. My suggestions are going unheeded. I just can't seem to understand where they are coming from."

"But it sounds like you have a great team to help you out," I offered. "Have you tried including some different team members in the requirements-gathering meetings to get some different perspectives? I'm sure someone can identify with your client."

"That's the thing. I can't find anyone else who can help me deal with this client. Johnny, Jake, Gary, Edward, Billy—they're all in the same boat as I am, feeling confused and frustrated."

"Hmm...it would appear that your hiring didn't go as well as you thought," I speculated.

"Why do you say that?" he asked, genuinely perplexed. "I really feel like I identified personally with all the people I ended up hiring. They're the best of the best!"

"Yes, but what exactly do you mean by 'best'?" I replied.

LESSON

To many people, "diversity" conjures up images of hiring inferior quality for the sake of meeting quotas. However, the focus on diversity is much more complicated. No company is going to jump onto the diversity bandwagon if there are not real business benefits. But companies have found there are, in fact, long-term business benefits associated with a diverse workforce.

Why is diversity awareness necessary at all? Let's assume your project team has an opening. You want to hire the best candidate available, right? Of course, looking for the "best" candidate can be a highly subjective matter. What does it mean to be the "best" candidate?

In many cases, there is a clear "best" candidate based on experience and skill level. However, if multiple candidates are equal in the aforementioned categories, the hiring manager tends to rate a person's qualifications using his own background as a measuring stick. After all, if a project manager has a certain background and ends up in the position he is in today, wouldn't it make sense for him to look for those same traits in another person? However, typically when the manager makes this type of subconscious decision, he also tends to pick a person that physically looks like him as well.

Project managers also want to make sure they hire someone that will get along with the rest of the team. Again, if there are multiple candidates with close qualifications, the project team may choose a candidate that is more like themselves.

If teams are left on their own, these natural biases tend to result in a like group of people hiring a similar candidate. In some organizations and on some projects, this results in a bias against workers of the opposite sex. In other businesses, there is a bias based on age, culture, and race.

Companies, especially large ones, have tried to formalize and standardize the recruiting and hiring process in a way that allows each candidate to be judged based on the same set of criteria. The goal of a standardized process is usually not to hire diverse workers. The goal is to remove as many of the subconscious biases as possible and to ensure that the most qualified candidate is hired.

In addition to just being fair to all candidates, diversity has the following benefits to your company and your project team:

- **Making better decisions**: People from the same types of backgrounds can have a tendency to think alike and this can affect the decisions that people make. Project managers need a diverse set of opinions to make the best technical decisions, to communicate more effectively with their clients, and to design and build the most creative solutions.

- **Hiring better people**: Ultimately, there is value in being able to hire the best person, regardless of the person's background. In many cases, organizations that do not value diversity end up hiring a group of people that all look and act the same. They will tell you that they are always hiring the "best." But is it really true that the "best" people all look and act the same? I don't think so. If the entire team looks and acts the same, I would assume you have not hired the best people. You have just hired clones of your current team.

- **Running better projects**: You have to be experienced at managing diverse people to excel in today's global marketplace. Can a project manager manage a worldwide distributed team if he has never managed people that are different than him? Can you service your diverse customer community effectively without a diverse project team? Managers will struggle to manage global projects if they don't have skills and experience with a diverse set of team members.

The bottom line is that there is value in having a diverse workforce and a diverse project team. If this was just an artificial feel-good idea, it would not be so important to so many companies. However, companies have found that valuing diversity results in hiring better people and providing real business benefit.

Define the Many Aspects of What Is In Scope and Out of Scope

I purposely scheduled all my meetings for the beginning of the day on February 14. I always bought Pam a dozen roses for Valentine's Day, and I wanted to leave work early to stop by the florist. I wanted to leave especially early today because I was also planning a romantic dinner for the evening. My last appointment was with Danielle Bartlett, a young, single woman who had been with the company for about four months.

She was wearing a black sweater and black pants, and she looked a little glum when she entered my office.

"Hey Danielle, good to see you," I said as she sat down. "What's with the all black today? You studying to become a Jedi Knight?"

Danielle smiled for a brief moment then slumped her shoulders back down. "Actually, Tom, I hate Valentine's Day," she said, trying again to smile. "Let me rephrase that: I hate being single on Valentine's Day!"

I nodded my head and smiled. Danielle seemed like a nice woman and I wanted to offer her some reassurance, but I didn't know her very well and I didn't think anything I said would make her feel better, so instead we talked about work. She was beginning the early stages of a construction cost-estimating package for the Facilities department, and she had e-mailed me a draft of her Project Charter document. I thought a few areas needed more work, including more definition and clarity around the project scope.

"Danielle, I've heard different people talk about the benefits of this cost estimating package and it seems like everyone has a different idea about what the final solution will look like. But when I read your scope statement, it left me with more questions than answers."

"I've defined the scope as best I know it," she replied. "I've stated that we will be implementing a tool to help estimate costs on major construction projects. It seems pretty clear to me."

"Well, I wonder if it is clear to the people reading the Project Charter," I said. "First of all, are you clear on whether the tool will be available worldwide or just in the U.S. division?"

"That's an easy one," she answered. "Other countries have different construction rules and regulations. Initially, we will use the tool only for U.S. construction projects. It may be customized for other countries later."

"Okay," I said. "Your business client is the Facilities department. But I've also heard that the tool might be of use in the Capital Accounting Group so they can allocate costs more effectively to the appropriate capital accounts."

Again, Danielle had the answer. "My sponsor said I didn't have to worry about the accounting implications. If they want to leverage the package, they will need to wait until the initial implementation is completed."

I had one more question to drive home the point. "I also heard that people like the idea of being able to use the tool on their laptop. Then they can enter information when they are at the construction site and update it in real time."

Danielle was starting to get the picture. "Actually, the standalone capability will be available in a subsequent upgrade product. By the way, I get your point. Given the different expectations people have for this project, I guess the original scope statement was pretty vague."

LESSON

Defining scope is perhaps the most important part of the project planning process. If you don't know what you are delivering and the boundaries of the project, you have no chance for success. In addition, if you have not done a good job of defining scope, managing scope will be almost impossible. Defining scope is not hard, but it does take an understanding of the components. Let's first think of scope in terms of high-level and low-level.

High-Level Scope: Deliverables and Boundaries

High-level scope is defined in the project planning process. There are two major aspects of defining scope on your project: deliverables and boundaries.

- **The deliverables:** If you are not sure of how to define scope on the project, you should at least include the deliverables (or products). Understanding the deliverables goes a long way toward understanding the scope of the project. You should focus on the final deliverables of the project first, and then any interim project deliverables that are especially important.
- **Project boundaries:** A project boundary is anything that can be expressed in terms of both an in-scope and out-of-scope statement. For example, Danielle is going to look for a tool that is to be used in the United States, but she is not considering the rest of the world. In this case, the United States is in scope and the rest of the world is out of scope. If she was considering the needs of the entire global company, this would not have been a good boundary statement since she could not have stated a good out-of-scope statement.

Once you have described the deliverables and the boundaries, you have completed high-level scope. This should be enough for the planning process.

Low-Level Scope: Requirements

Knowing the deliverables and perhaps a short description will not be enough for you to actually build the deliverables. You need something else: *requirements* (also called *specifications*). Think about what the requirements are—they are actually nothing more than a detailed description of your deliverables. Requirements can be broken up into two categories: features and functions.

- **Features (product requirements)** describe the physical charac-teristics of the deliverables. If you were building a bridge, for in-stance, most of the requirements would be features. These might include the number of cars the bridge will hold, the strength of the steel, the length of the span, etc.
- **Functions (process requirements)** describe how people inter-act with a deliverable and how a deliverable interacts with other deliverables. For example, if you need to change invoicing and billing transactions, most of the requirements could end up being process oriented. This would include how billing transactions move from orders to invoicing to accounts receivable.

Together, the features and functions define the project deliverables in more detail. The deliverables are understood early in the project and help make up high-level scope. The detailed requirements describe the deliverables in more detail. The requirements make up low-level scope. In fact, once the project starts executing, most scope change requests will end up being changes to requirements.

Danielle's scope statement is very typical of how some project managers de-fine project scope. It is brief and to the point, but it also leaves questions in the minds of readers. Remember, the purpose of defining scope is to clearly articulate what you are taking responsibility for delivering on the project. You don't want to define your project, gain sponsor approval, and then have questions arise later about exactly what is included in your project.

Based on the little I know of Danielle's project, I have already identified three areas where she should further clarify what is in scope and out of scope—and there may still be more areas. The good news is she knows the information. However, she is not sharing the information nor being clear to the reader. She should be much clearer about what locations and organizations will be included in the initial deployment. Because there is some confusion in other related organizations, she should state specifically that the accounting group and other groups are out of scope. She should also be clear about the major features and capabilities that will and will not be included. The scope statement is not the place to put requirements, but the question of whether the solution can be used with a laptop sounds like it is an area of potential confusion. By being clear in the high-level scope definition, Danielle can better manage expectations and the change process during the project.

Why is this discussion on project scope important? It's important because a lack of scope is one of the primary causes of problems on projects. Although there are a number of causes for poorly managing scope on a project, one of the primary causes is that the scope was never defined well in the beginning. It is impossible to manage project scope if it's never defined and approved. Now that you better understand the components of scope, you will be in a position to make sure projects define scope well. Then you can manage change effectively. This does not mean that changes cannot occur. It means that change is recognized and managed.

Use the "Big Three" Documents

Project Charter, Project Schedule, and Requirements as the Foundation for Your Project

I pulled our car slowly into the driveway on Baker Street and squinted at the front door in an attempt to determine if this was indeed Wayne's house. Pam and I had been here several times before, but the house next to Wayne's looked similar from the outside and I always got them confused. The Morettis had invited us and another couple over for dinner, and we were early, as usual. I grabbed the bottle of wine from the back seat and we headed toward the front door.

Wayne greeted us and led us into the kitchen where his wife Elsie was busy cooking. The Morettis' house was warm and cozy, a combination of old world charm and modern-day conveniences. Wayne liked to have the newest gadgets and gizmos, and his home certainly reflected it. He took the most pride in showing off his basement, complete with plasma TV, pinball machine, pool table, bar, leather recliners, and fireplace. His collection of beer steins was prominently displayed on several walls and shelves.

Wayne had just opened our bottle of wine when the doorbell rang. Elsie greeted the new guests and brought them into the kitchen where Wayne introduced them as the Henleys—Patrick and Carolyn. Patrick was a manager in the finance division at our company and Carolyn was a kindergarten teacher. Wayne asked all of us to sit around the dining room table and talk, while Elsie brought out several appetizers. She also poured glasses of wine for the Henleys.

Patrick and I sat next to each other at the table and, after a bit of small talk, began discussing his job. It turned out he was responsible for managing a project to implement new finance procedures for the Accounting department. The work had been going on for three months.

Obviously, his work struck a chord with me and I was excited to learn more.

"The project has taken longer than I originally estimated," Patrick admitted. "We seem to be trying to hit a moving target. First, we were just going to implement some additional auditing processes. Then we were asked to update the company chart of accounts. Now they want us to standardize the entire auditing process. The original project was estimated to take two months. My manager keeps asking me when the work will be done, but how can I know when they keep adding more? She is anxious for us to finish so she can start us on a new project of interest to her."

"Interesting," I replied. "Given the three months you have invested already, and the changes you have picked up, how much of the project is left to complete?"

"Well, that depends on the accounting users," he explained. "If they accept our team's recommendations for the auditing process, the work might be completed in another two months or so. However, based on what we have done so far, the target always seems to be changing. Just as we think we are making progress, we find out something else needs to change. Just last week, for instance, we found out that the auditors now want us to compare our auditing practices against others in our industry."

"Do you have anything written down describing what you are doing or what your client is asking for?"

I knew the answer before I asked the question. "No," he said.

Again, I thought of Jerry and Susan. Looks like they "don't do projects" in Patrick's area either.

LESSON

Processes associated with managing a project have little value if you don't know what you are delivering and how you are going to do it. That is why the upfront definition and planning processes are so valuable. You can be the greatest workload manager in the world, but you are going to fail if you don't have agreement on what you are delivering and what it takes to get the work done. There are three major documents that build this foundation for a project: the project charter, the project schedule, and the business requirements.

The project charter defines the project deliverables, scope, assumptions, risks, costs, timelines, approach, etc. It is absolutely vital to have this document in place before you start the project work. This does not have to be a 30-page document. Scalability is still the rule. Small projects may be defined in a couple of pages. Enhancement requests might need just one page. Larger projects need more planning information and will have a longer charter. It is important to gain agreement with your sponsor on the work to be accomplished. If you can't easily gain consensus on what the project is delivering, then it is even more vital that the work waits until agreement is reached. The project charter also communicates the project essentials to other stakeholders for their agreement and feedback.

The project schedule describes how you will execute the project, including building and deploying the deliverables. You may be able to plan out the activities for a small project in your head. However, as projects get larger, the schedule needs to be documented in a tool of some kind. The schedule allows you to estimate the overall timeline and helps you see the critical path of work driving the deadline.

Once the schedule is built, it must be kept current so that you can tell whether you are falling behind. An updated schedule also tells you how much work remains to complete the project.

The business requirements describe in more detail the characteristics, features, and functions of the deliverables. The project charter describes the main deliverables of the project as part of the project scope. However, the details and characteristics of the deliverables are not in the project charter.

Normally, this level of detail is not known when the project charter is created. The business requirements describe the details of the deliverables so that you can design and build them correctly. Gaining approval on this document also ensures that a common set of expectations with the business client exists. If you don't have defined and approved requirements, you will find it difficult to manage scope effectively.

Looking at Patrick's project, it is clear he has not yet established the project foundation. He has no charter, schedule, or requirements. Consequently, he is not able to control scope (which would be in the project charter), he does not know how much work is required to complete the deliverables (from the schedule), and he is not sure how to build the deliverables (from the business requirements). It is not possible to know how much work is left or whether he is on the right track. Without these three "friends" he will be lost.

Given the track record of the project so far, the best advice for Patrick is to pause the project and quickly write up the project charter, schedule, and requirements documents. This will validate whether Patrick and his sponsor are in agreement on the work, what that work looks like, and how much time and effort it will take to accomplish the work. If he is on the right track, he should be able to resume his work and take the project to completion. If he is not on the right track, the sponsor can decide whether the work should proceed given the effort required to get it back on track. Right now, no one can make an informed decision since there is no agreed-upon information on which to base a decision.

Use Scope Change Management

To Allow the Sponsor to Make the Final Decision (Many Times The Sponsor Will Say "No")

Jerry and I met on February 22 in my office to discuss his phone mail project and his housing situation with the Morettis. Jerry and Barbara had visited Wayne and Elsie several times since our initial meeting and house tour, and Jerry and Wayne had begun talking about the price. Jerry seemed energized by his housing success, and he thanked me repeatedly for connecting him with Wayne. We talked at great length about his plans for moving in over the summer, and he made a special point of telling me that Wayne had agreed to leave his pool table and pinball machine as housewarming gifts.

If left unchecked, Jerry would have probably talked forever about the house, but eventually I focused his attention on work-related matters.

After four weeks of work, the phone mail system was going through some initial pilot testing.

"As we have been checking the phones and the wiring, we have also been working on the new voicemail software. We have the software in pilot test now and the test is going smoothly," Jerry began. "But yesterday we received a request to change the call forwarding feature. The pilot team says it is more confusing to use than the old version, and they want the old functionality back."

"If I remember your project charter, you stated you were going to implement the new upgrade as is, with no custom modifications," I replied. "If your clients are requesting changes to the software, it sounds like a change request to me."

"You're right," Jerry agreed, "but it's not only a scope change—it's also a distraction. The vendor's first estimate is that the change will take two extra weeks and cost us around $10,000. Then we will have to retest to make sure nothing else is broken. In addition, this slightly customized version of the software may cause us more problems down the road. I really wish we didn't have to do it."

I was sympathetic to Jerry's concerns, but I had an idea where this would all end up. "I don't think your situation is as bad as you think," I suggested. "You have enough information about the impact on the project to talk to your sponsor. First, make sure she is willing to proceed with the change."

"Good idea," Jerry said hopefully. "I'll try to have a short meeting with her this afternoon."

Later that day Jerry called me. "Well, I just had a great meeting with the sponsor," he said in an upbeat tone.

"And what did she say about making the change the pilot team recommended?" I asked.

"She emphatically told me 'Forget about it!'" Jerry replied, sounding more relaxed. "She said the new upgrade might be different, and it may not be perfect, but it's good enough!"

Just as I thought, I said to myself.

LESSON

There are two major reasons why projects have problems. The first is a basic lack of upfront definition and planning. The second is poor scope change management processes. Remember that scope refers to the box that defines the work of your project. High-level scope includes deliverables and boundary statements. The business requirements make up lower-level scope. Defining scope allows you to ensure you have an agreement with your sponsor on the box your project is responsible for. Defining scope also provides the baseline against which you can perform scope change management throughout the project.

Scope change management is necessary to protect the initial agreement you have with the sponsor. In the project charter, you agree to deliver a certain set of products for a certain level of effort, cost, and duration. If the basic nature of the products change, it is reasonable to expect the associated cost, effort, and time to complete the work may change as well.

One of the conflicts project managers face is that they don't want to say "no" to someone who asks for a scope change. The requestor could be a client manager, stakeholder, or end user. If the requestor asks for changes, the project manager usually feels an instinct to say, "Yes, we can do it." Somehow, saying "no" to the request is seen as not being client focused or not satisfying the client's needs.

The beauty of scope change management, however, is that the project manager does not have to be the "no" guy. In fact, the project manager does not need to decide one way or another—that is not the job of a project manager. The project manager's job is to identify the request and take it through the scope change management process. This includes evaluating the impact of the change on the project, looking at alternatives, and taking the information to the project sponsor for resolution.

Sponsors should make decisions on scope changes because it is their project and ultimately they're the ones that need to live with the results. The sponsor and the project team set expectations in the signed project charter. This is further clarified in the approved business requirements. These are the expectations that are in place. If people have requests for changes to these agreements, the sponsor needs to make the decision on whether to approve the change or not. This decision should be based on the business value provided and the overall impact on the project in terms of cost, delivery time, or quality.

The sponsor also has the added advantage of organizational power. Although it is sometimes hard for the project team to say "no" to the client, the sponsor doesn't have that problem. Clients and end users usually work in the sponsor's organization. Since the sponsor is paying for the project, they are usually more concerned about it completing as promised within the budget and delivery date.

This change in expectations may be fine. The sponsor may ask your team to change the project scope and also agree to the corresponding change in effort, cost, and scope. However, this is not a given—especially if the changes are very large or very small.

Jerry's sponsor is typical. She didn't have much patience for changes in scope resulting in marginal benefit. Small changes viewed as critical to the end users usually pale when viewed from the sponsor's perspective. On the other hand, if the change is important enough, the sponsor can provide the incremental budget and timeline required to complete the extra work. A side benefit of going to the sponsor is that after invoking the process once or twice, fewer scope change requests come up. People are much less likely to request changes without a very good business case if they realize the sponsor is actively evaluating all of these requests.

Collect Metrics

To Evaluate How Well You (and Your Project) Are Performing

I had been working as project management advisor for almost two full months now and I was interested in some feedback regarding my performance in this new role. My boss Wayne agreed to talk with some of his management peers to see if they had heard anything from their staff. Our meeting today was to discuss this feedback.

I entered Wayne's office around 3 p.m. and found him poking his finger at a shiny new tablet. "New iPad?" I asked. "Yes, indeed," he replied. "I bought it last night on my way home from work. Still getting use to the keyboard on the screen, though."

Wayne put his iPad down on a stack of paperwork on his desk, then opened his desk drawer and pulled out a brochure and handed it to me, smiling. "Desert Oasis" is sprawled in fancy italic type across the front, with overlapping photos of a golf course, pool, and an elderly couple enjoying lunch.

"What's this?" I asked.

"Our new home," he replied. Wayne mentioned a few weeks ago how he and Elsie were going to move to a warmer climate this summer after his retirement and how a friend had recommended the Desert Oasis resort. Apparently, he and Elsie had flown to Arizona last October and toured the property. The tone of his voice told me he was excited.

Of course, I was happy for Wayne and his wife. But I knew it would be tough seeing him retire and move away. In fact, after a few weeks of reflection, I was still somewhat in shock.

Wayne sat down in the big leather chair in front of his desk and gestured for me to take a seat. Putting the brochure back in the drawer, he pulled out a file folder and sat back contentedly.

"Well, I've got more good news, Tom," he started. "I spoke with four managers and all the feedback on your job performance was positive. Even your friend Jerry put together a decent project charter and schedule. In the past, he would have been a third of the way to disaster by now."

"That's great to hear," I said. "But was there any other feedback?"

"Not really. Just a lot of positive comments"

"Well, the feedback is nice, and I believe I am on the right track, but right now this is just 'feel-good' feedback. I guess it's time I start to collect some more meaningful data on the value I'm providing."

"Value?" Wayne questioned. "The feedback I received was that you have been providing a lot of value."

"Yes, and I appreciate the kind words. But the feedback is from fellow managers whom you have worked with for years. I hope their kind words are true, but I need to collect some more meaningful, quantitative comments on the value I am providing. I'm preaching the value of collecting metrics to the project managers I am working with—I guess I need to start taking some of my own medicine."

LESSON

What if a publicly-traded company could not tell a shareholder its revenues or profits for the fiscal year? That company would have some serious problems to address. Likewise, if the same shareholder asked a company executive how its products were viewed in the marketplace, and he replied only with a "good," that would not be very comforting for the shareholder, either.

The preceding examples never happen, though, because companies collect metrics. They collect financial information on revenue and costs, and they collect data on how their products are perceived in the marketplace. For good or for bad, they typically know much of the information they need to run the business.

On a much smaller scale, a stakeholder might ask you how successful a recent project was, or how efficient a billing process is, or, in my case, what value I am providing with my coaching service. These questions are usually harder to answer.

Many (probably most) companies have no idea whether they are getting value for the dollars they spend on projects, and they have only a vague idea about the success of individual projects. Defining and collecting an appropriate set of metrics is the only way to get quantitative and qualitative information. Collecting metrics provides the information necessary to improve processes and gives results that show if expectations are being met.

My situation is a good example. I am providing a service to the organization, but I need to collect information to show the effectiveness and value of the service I provide to project managers. I can't just rely on anecdotal comments from high-level managers. I need more facts and should be collecting metrics in the following areas:

- The number of project managers I am assisting, both current month and year-to-date.
- A satisfaction survey asking project managers about my service level and the value (or lack of value) I added to their projects.
- A survey question about whether I kept my commitments within the agreed-upon time frame.
- Any quantifiable numbers in terms of cost or time savings that can be attributed to my services.

My job represents one small component of the entire organization. All teams should be collecting metrics. If an organization is not familiar with collecting metrics, the basic philosophy should be to just start collecting them—even if they turn out to be the wrong ones. It is important to start collecting some metrics—and to modify them over time if they don't provide indications of how effective and successful a project or process is. Metrics are the best way to quantitatively show if you (or your project) are improving and whether you have truly met expectations.

Give Performance Feedback Routinely

Not Just During Formal Reviews

My last appointment on the last day of February was with Miles O'Brien. Miles grew up in New York and was the oldest brother in a large Irish family. He had curly red hair, a white complexion, and bright green eyes. Miles was perhaps best known for his office attire on St. Patrick's Day. Every year he came to work dressed in a bright green suit and tie with a green top hat. I had been meeting with him on an ad-hoc basis to talk about his project to install a new release of the company's contract management application for the Purchasing Department. He came by my office around 4 p.m.

"How are you, Miles?" I asked as he entered my office.

"I'm a little hungry, but otherwise things are great."

"I've got some leftover snacks from my lunch today. Would you like some crackers with peanut butter?"

"No thanks, Tom. I'm actually on a diet. I need to lose about ten pounds before St. Patrick's Day or I won't be able to fit into my suit."

"In that case, we better get you some donuts and candy!" I replied with a chuckle.

"Oh, c'mon! Are you telling me you don't like my green suit?" Miles said with a smile. He told me he tried it on several weeks ago and noticed the pants were a bit snug, which was why he needed to shed a few pounds. He was trying a low-carb diet in the hopes of losing the weight quickly.

"Not to be morbid, Miles, but didn't the inventor of that low-carb diet pass away a few years back? Maybe it's not a good diet plan after all."

"Not sure about that, Tom," he replied. "Truth is I am just trying to shed a few pounds quickly, and a friend of mine told me low-carbing it would do the trick."

"Well, best of luck to you," I said as we both sat down. "Why don't you fill me in on your project's status?"

"We were testing the new release of our package when we discovered a major problem in one of the components," he began. "This testing was assigned to a team member but he seems to have missed the problem."

"It's too bad you discovered the problem so late in the project," I said, "but at least you found it."

"To be honest, Tom, we've been having testing problems for quite a while now. Arthur, the team member assigned to this work, has missed a number of problems. He is probably not the best person for the job, but everyone on the project already has a full plate, so the task fell to him."

"Well, I'm assuming he has testing experience," I said.

"Yes, he has the experience but it's not his favorite thing to do, so I don't think he's motivated. I think he can do better, but he's getting sloppy and cutting corners. I have already made a note to discuss this with him at his next performance review. Hopefully the problem will resolve itself before long."

"Miles, repeated mistakes from anyone deserve immediate attention," I explained to him. "I don't think you can afford to wait until Arthur's performance review."

LESSON

The world is made up of people with various skills and talents. Often, people's talents drive them to work in certain areas where they excel. In other cases, the individual talents and the jobs they perform are not aligned. Sometimes this lack of alignment can be overcome with hard work and motivation. Unfortunately, sometimes the gap can't be overcome. These are the times when you have to deal with the individual as a performance problem.

As a project manager, you don't usually have total management control over your team members. Usually you share responsibility with the team member's functional manager. However, this doesn't mean that you are powerless to work with team members that are not meeting expectations. In fact, you have an obligation. Developing and managing team members are key responsibilities of a project manager—at least over the duration of the project.

How do you deal with team members that are not meeting expectations? Try this approach.

- **Give immediate feedback**: Performance feedback should be given immediately after you observe a problem. Giving the feedback immediately allows it to have maximum impact.
- **Gather your facts:** Feedback should not be generic or vague. It also should not be based on what someone else said. The feedback should be based on your own observations. For instance, if the person is not meeting his deadlines, you should have multiple examples that you can point to. If you think a person is disruptive, you should have specific instances where you observed this behavior.
- **Meet in person**: Once the factual examples are ready, have a preliminary performance discussion. There are three targeted objectives to this meeting:

  - To make the employee aware of the perceived performance problem. To be fair, he or she may not realize that there is a problem.
  - To get the employee's feedback and response to your observations.

- To determine a short-term action plan. This is critical and will be the key to turning the performance around.

  This discussion is valuable for both the project manager and the team member.

- **Escalate to the functional manager:** In most cases, this preliminary, fact-based discussion is enough to turn the situation around. There is no need for follow-up. However, if the problems continue, your next course of action is to bring this situation to the attention of the team member's functional manager. The functional manager can provide further guidance and may well have to get involved to try to resolve the problem. For some team members this might mean being removed from the project team, setting up a performance plan, or even being fired. These are options available to the functional manager that are usually not available to the project manager.

One of the most difficult aspects of being a project manager is that you often (always?) have limited functional control over your team members. This makes it difficult to respond when people do not perform to your expectations. Resolving performance problems on your team may not be totally in your control, but you don't have to give up, either. You do have options. You need to work with the team member first to try to resolve the situation between the two of you, and then escalate the problem to the functional manager if necessary.

Ensure Issues Management Is Everyone's Responsibility

March arrived in Dickens with a bang. A large cold front from the north created a snowstorm that deposited another three inches of fresh snow on the ground. Pam was very busy at work preparing for the men's college basketball conference tournament, which was being hosted by Northeast Illinois State. I was busy painting our living room, replacing the kitchen tile, and helping people manage projects at work.

My first meeting on Monday was with Mike Miller, whose project was to install document management software in the Legal department. Mike and I had driven to Chicago two weekends ago to catch a Bulls game, and we were quickly becoming good friends. After three months in my role as project management advisor, I began to realize that I had very few friends to talk to about my own work. Most of my friends were colleagues from the office, and when we got together it was so they could talk to me about how work was going for them.

Mike, however, was always eager to listen and always seemed to have something insightful and meaningful to say. He was also a big sports fan, and we could spend hours debating who was the best NFL quarterback of all time. He liked Joe Montana from the 49ers, but I preferred Johnny Unitas of the Baltimore Colts—old "Johnny Hightops."

When he arrived at my door, I was surprised to find him holding what appeared to be a gift. "It's for you," he said as he handed me the box. "Open it." I tore the paper from the box and opened it slowly, trying to add some dramatic flair. As I pushed the tissue paper aside, a smile formed across my face and I let out a loud laugh. It was a Joe Montana jersey.

"I thought you might get a kick out of that!" he said as he closed my office door.

"That's great, Mike. Thanks a lot! Although I'm not quite sure what to do with it!"

"Maybe you can re-gift it to me," Mike said as he took a seat and pulled out his project folder from his briefcase. At the Bulls game, Mike mentioned his project was going very smoothly. I remembered him saying his team had not yet encountered any major problems. In fact, they were scheduled to begin testing the software last week.

"Well, Mike, you almost completed the project without any hassle. But it sounds like something came up."

"You're right, Coach. I shouldn't have told you how smoothly things were going. Looks like I jinxed myself!"

"What's the trouble?"

"A problem was uncovered late in our project," he began. "It turns out the document management software doesn't interface well with one of our existing legacy systems, which is causing the legacy system to lock up on a regular basis."

"That's a surprise," I replied. "What kind of feedback have you been getting from the team members doing the testing?"

"That's the frustrating part. I've been getting periodic updates from them and they've never mentioned this problem. The team said they thought they could resolve it on their own."

"Have you notified your clients?" I asked.

I could tell he was frustrated. "You are not going to believe this, but the clients already knew about the problem! Since they were helping to test the old system, they were the ones who discovered the problem to begin with."

"So, most of the team knew, except you," I concluded. "Many technical people are natural problem solvers. They probably thought they could resolve this on their own. They also may have felt that raising an issue would have generated scrutiny of their work. They may not understand that issues management raises the visibility of a problem so it can be resolved quickly."

"Two weeks ago, we probably could have resolved this and still met our project timeline. Now, the resolution may cause the end date to slip."

LESSON

All projects encounter problems. In fact, for a larger project, there may be people talking to the project manager every day about one type of problem or another. These are not issues. Most are just typical problems requiring quick decisions to be made from one or more decent alternatives. At other times, there may not even be a problem involved. For example, it may be a team member just doesn't know how to respond to a certain situation.

On the other hand, a formal issue is a problem that will impede the progress of the project because it cannot be entirely resolved by the project team. In other words, an issue is a big deal. It is a problem requiring special project management processes, including:

- Proactive communication with the client, sponsor, team members, and other interested stakeholders.
- Consistent and ongoing follow-up to ensure the issue is resolved as quickly as possible.
- Special problem-solving techniques if the issue is not easy to understand or address.

Sometimes when project team members hear about issues management, they think project management processes don't apply to them. After all, project management processes are for project managers, right? Wrong! To be successful, the entire team needs to understand that they are all part of the process. For issues management, one of their primary responsibilities is to raise issues when they see them. This responsibility isn't limited to the project team. All stakeholders should surface and escalate any issues they encounter.

Raising an issue isn't a negative. It is a proactive way to identify a problem so the team can apply appropriate resources, find alternatives, and implement a resolution. On a large project, for instance, you may have a fairly rigorous process for managing issues. This entire process could look something like the following:

1. Solicit potential issues from any project stakeholders, including the project team, clients, sponsors, etc. An issue can be surfaced through verbal or written means, but it must be formally documented using an Issue Submission Form. This form includes a description of the issue, the impact to the project, potential resolutions, recommended course of action, who should be involved in resolving the issues, and more.

2. Enter the issue into the Issues Log for tracking purposes.

3. Assign the issue to a project team member for investigation (project managers could assign it to themselves). The team member will investigate options that are available to resolve the issue. For each option, he or she should also estimate the impact to the project in terms of budget, schedule, and scope.

4. The various alternatives and impact to the problem are documented on the Issue Submission Form. Take the issue, alternatives, and project impact on the Issue Submission Form to the appropriate stakeholders for a resolution. The actual people that are involved in resolving the issue are the same ones that were identified on the Issue Submission Form.

5. Document the resolution or course of action on the Issue Submission Form.

6. Document the issue resolution briefly on the Issues Log.

7. Make the appropriate adjustments to the project schedule and budget, if necessary.

8. If the resolution of an issue causes the project budget or duration to change, the current project charter may need to be updated.

9. Communicate issue status and resolutions to project team members and other appropriate stakeholders through the Manage Communication process, including the Project Status Report.

On Mike's project, team members discovered a problem and thought they could resolve it on their own. This is an admirable first step. You don't want to raise an issue for a problem the team can resolve itself. However, when the initial resolution attempts did not succeed, they should have raised this problem with Mike. Mike might have had other ideas on how to resolve the problem before it became an issue. If those ideas did not work, Mike could have raised a formal issue, which would have invoked a proactive issues management process. Since a third-party package was involved, the problem may not have been within the team's control to resolve. The team could have identified options to resolve the problem, suggested workarounds, or changed the project scope with the sponsor to make the issue irrelevant. Of course, all of these options are still available now. However, it may be too late to complete the project by the deadline date since the issue was not raised in a timely manner.

Shorten Long Meetings to Sharpen the Focus

I had just finished setting up another meeting with Jerry Ackerman when Ashley Parker walked into my office. We were going to lunch together to discuss her project, and she was a little early. There was a nice Italian restaurant, Mama Leoni's, a few miles south of our office, and we decided to go together in Ashley's SUV. It beats eating peanut butter and crackers at my desk any time.

Mama Leoni's was a family establishment built in the 1950s; it was renovated in the 1980s but still retained the original leather booths. Anthony and Tina Leoni, the owners, still cooked on occasion, but Anthony, Jr., the Leoni's oldest son, now handled the day-to-day management of the restaurant. The building had withstood both fire and flood during its 30-year history but had never closed for longer than two months.

It was March and I had not seen Ashley since early January when she was struggling with a sponsor who had been reassigned during her project. I knew she had been able to gain agreement from her new sponsor on the work required for the next phase of her project, so we had not had reason to talk since. After ordering lunch, we got down to business.

"So, what's the latest, Ashley? Everything okay with your new sponsor?"

"Oh yes, he's a great person. He's very professional and very thorough."

"Sounds great. How can I help you then?"

Ashley began discussing her project. She was having trouble with her status meetings, which she held once a week with her clients and team members. She said she was having a hard time covering everything on the agenda in two hours.

"Your status meetings are two hours?" I asked, surprised. "Tell me more. What does your agenda look like?"

Ashley went over the contents of the meeting matter-of-factly, counting off the items that she and her team discussed on her fingers—an update on the project and schedule, a discussion of the action items from the previous meetings, outstanding issues, and change requests. People could also add other small items to the agenda as needed.

"The agenda sounds good," I said. "Where do you think the meeting is breaking down?"

"I think the team tries to do too much problem solving during the meeting. We end up spending all of our time hashing and rehashing many of the same items from week to week. We also tend to get side-tracked, and it seems like we can never finish the meeting on time. Some members of the team think we need to lengthen the meetings to two-and-a-half or three hours."

"I have a better idea," I said quickly. "To get your meeting more focused and to better utilize everyone's time, don't add more time—reduce it instead. Cut the meeting back from two hours to one."

LESSON

Status meetings are essential to ensure that the project team and the client maintain healthy and open communication and to ensure everyone's expectations are in sync. Even many of the light agile project methodologies rely on frequent, short team meetings to share information and status. A traditional status meeting usually includes the project team members. The meeting can also include clients (the people gaining the benefit of the project) and perhaps even the sponsor. Because many of the project decision makers are there, these meetings may seem like a good time to resolve open issues and action items.

In a large company like Mega Manufacturing, it can be difficult to get the right people focused and on the same page for decision making. If you can get all of them into a meeting, the temptation is to use that time to discuss and resolve problems. Unfortunately, this may result in people delaying their day-to-day decisions and instead bringing items to the status meeting for discussion and resolution. This diverts from the main purpose of the meeting and may result in less urgency in the day-to-day work environment.

On the surface, this might not seem too bad. After all, the right people are there. Why not engage in problem-solving and decision-making activities? The problem is that this is not the purpose of the status meeting. The purpose is to keep everyone up to date with what is going on, at a level where the information is of interest to all (or almost all) of the participants. In addition to a recap of project status, items such as change requests, issues, or new risks should be discussed because they could impact everyone.

Bringing routine items to the status meeting for resolution will cause the meeting to break down—just as Ashley is experiencing. Small problems or questions that impact only a few people end up being discussed by a subset of the team. As the questions change, different people get engaged, but not everyone is involved. In a two-hour meeting, each person may only be actively participating for 30 to 45 minutes, and then wishing they were somewhere else for the remainder. Of course, not everyone can be actively engaged for the entire meeting, but 45 minutes out of a one-hour meeting is much better than 45 minutes out of a two-hour meeting.

As the project manager, Ashley can and should change the format and the agenda of the meeting. More than anyone else, she is responsible for making sure people's time is treated valuably. If she is not careful, people will start to complain that they are wasting their time, and they will begin to skip the meetings.

The good news is that Ashley seems to understand the meetings are not effective in their current format. She knows they are not able to cover all of the important business because they are spending too much time problem solving. Her solution to extend the meeting seems appropriate, but it will cause even greater problems. Instead, she should use shorter meetings to force the team to be more focused. This will require better planning for the meeting, including communicating discussion items before the meeting starts.

It would be wrong to imply that no decision making can occur at a status meeting. Decision making regarding issues, risks, and changes is perfectly acceptable. If everyone knows what topics will be covered ahead of time, they can discuss them rapidly and resolve them quickly. If it becomes clear that a quick and easy resolution is not possible, then further discussion and decision making needs to be tabled and resolved offline.

The project manager normally acts as the meeting facilitator at a status meeting and is responsible for making sure the meeting is relevant and does not get side-tracked. So, while Ashley is certainly frustrated by how the meetings are turning out, she is also responsible for controlling the agenda and making sure the discussion stays on track.

Ashley must be firm in keeping the discussion on point. These may be valuable conversations, but they are usually not appropriate for the status meeting. Items need to be identified, taken offline, and resolved in another forum. One option for her to consider is to reduce the formal status meeting to one hour and keep the second hour open for any members who need further time for discussion. The people who were not impacted would be free to leave.

In general, longer meetings can leave numerous opportunities to wander. Short meetings force more focus on the areas needing coverage.

Identify the Root Cause of Problems

Jade Johnson was an older woman with curly black hair and a big nose. As far as I knew, she had never been married and still lived in an old house on Rutherford Street she bought more than 25 years ago. In my 10-plus years at Mega Manufacturing, I hadn't been able to find anyone who knew much about her, which was strange because she could tell you the life story, including the latest gossip, of everyone in the office.

In fact, it was spooky how much she knew about people. My first meeting with Jade was memorable. My wife and I had just moved to Dickens and it was only my second day on the job. A colleague introduced us when we bumped into her by the vending machines in the break room. The first thing she said to me was, "So, you're the one who bought that house on Wood Ranch. Tell me, how do you and Pam like the place?" I remember feeling an odd sensation in my stomach. I had never met this woman before, and yet she knew where I lived and my wife's name. A few months later, I discovered one of her sources: she sometimes ate lunch with a woman in Human Resources. Ten years later and I was still very careful with what I said around her.

She stopped by my office early Tuesday morning to discuss an issue she was having on her project to add an accounts receivable interface with another bank.

"Hello, Tom. How are you today?" she said in a raspy voice.

"I'm doing fine. Sounds like you have a cold."

"Just getting over one, actually. So, I hear you hooked up Jerry with the Morettis' place. I was surprised to find out Wayne is leaving Dickens. Tell me, where are he and his wife moving? Someplace south?"

I stared blankly into her face and shrugged my shoulders. I knew Wayne was going to Arizona, but I didn't know if it was common knowledge yet. If I told Jade, I knew it soon would be. She turned her head slightly to the right and squinted her eyes as she stared back at me for several seconds. Finally, she sat down and turned her focus to her project, which came as quite a relief to me.

Jade said her project required a number of changes to the interface files going to and coming from our main bank. She told me she was frustrated because the support staff at the bank was not available to help her team resolve a data transmission problem. My first question was whether she tried escalating the issue at the bank.

"I guess that's the next step," she replied, tapping her long nails on my desk. "But they have really been difficult to work with. This is the third time I have escalated problems because their staff is unavailable. They must hate to hear from me by now."

I perked up. "This is interesting," I said. "Whenever I see a pattern, it makes me think a symptom of the problem is being resolved rather than the root cause. Why are the bank people unavailable?"

"They are allocated to other projects and are too busy to help us with our problems."

"Okay, but why are the bank people allocated to other work?"

"Well, I was told they have a huge workload. Their people all get fully allocated, which means it's hard for us to get help when we need it."

"Wait a minute," I said. "We are making a major change to our interface. We should be a part of their workload. Why aren't they allocating resources to us?"

Jade thought for a minute, and the nail tapping stopped as she realized the answer.

LESSON

As you saw earlier, issues are major problems that will impede the progress of a project—problems not totally within the ability of the project team to resolve. Every issue has cause(s) and every issue has effect(s) on the project. Some complex issues also have symptoms, which outwardly may look like a cause, but are not actually at the root-cause level. Symptoms are directly or indirectly related to the problem, but are not the cause of the problem itself. A symptom is actually more of an effect of the problem.

Sometimes, in the heat of the battle, the project manager sees the effect an issue has on the project and looks quickly at the cause. In some cases, this first attempt at problem resolution actually addresses and fixes the cause. However, in other cases, the resolution only addresses a symptom, rather than the actual root cause. In many cases, resolving a symptom might, in fact, be good enough. The issue may go away and not return. However, if another similar issue arises later, it might mean that a more fundamental resolution is required.

Let's look again at Jade's problem. Since her initiative requires major changes to the bank interface, she should have involved the bank staff in the planning process. However, she neglected to do so. If her team had not experienced any problems, this lack of planning might not have been a problem. However, the interface is complicated, and the team has run into a number of problems.

When her team hit the first problem, Jade realized the bank was not very responsive. However, she did not think the problem through to find the root cause of the response-time problem. Her initial assumption was probably that they were not responsive because they did not have a good customer service mindset. But it turns out this is not the case.

The way to get to the root cause is by asking a series of "why" questions. After asking a series of "why" questions, Jade would have realized the bank support staff was unavailable because they were allocated to other projects and other clients. Jade did not communicate with the bank about her project and her potential support needs. Escalating the support issue at the bank only resolved the symptom at the time, which was that their staff was unavailable.

Jade resolved the particular problem she faced the first time, but she did not get to the root cause. Unfortunately, the problem did not go away for good. A little later a similar problem occurred with the bank's allocation of their staffing resources. Again, Jade resolved the particular problem facing her team at that time by escalating the lack of support staffing, but she did not resolve the root cause. Since this was the second time this problem occurred, Jade should have realized that her first attempt at problem resolution did not resolve the root cause of this problem.

So now she is bringing this to my attention. When I first hear the problem, I also jump toward resolving the symptom by escalating the problem once again at the bank. However, when Jade says this is the third time the problem has occurred, I know the root cause is not being addressed. The bank can't be responsive because the support staff is allocated to other customers. They are not allocated to Jade's project because she did not include them in her planning. Therefore, the bank doesn't know of her testing needs and didn't allocate any support resources to her project. Her best option now is to work with the support manager at the bank to get a person assigned to this project to help her team when they have problems. This should resolve the root cause of the problem.

Use Quality Assurance to Validate Project Status

I bought my son Tim a special set of Mickey Mouse golf clubs last Christmas, and he seemed to enjoy swinging them in the backyard when the weather allowed and in the basement when the weather didn't. The first week of April brought mild temperatures, so on the first sunny day I took Tim to play his first round of miniature golf. In my opinion, he putted fairly well for a youngster, although I wasn't sure if he enjoyed putting the ball into the hole as much as through the clown's nose or over the bumps and hills. I hoped he wouldn't be disappointed when he went to his first real golf course and didn't find any windmills or concrete banks off of which to bounce his ball.

I was telling the story of our day on the miniature links to Marketing Manager Bailey Jenkins, who had been working with Ashley on the Marketing information database project. Ashley and I had met a few times to discuss this project, but this was my first time meeting with Bailey. I knew Bailey was really into meditation because I heard nature CDs playing in her office the last time I visited with Ashley, who explained that Bailey likes to meditate during her lunch hour.

"I tell you, Bailey, he might just be the next Tiger Woods!" I said, finishing my story about Tim and miniature golfing.

"Well, you know, Tom, Tiger did get his start in golf at about the same age as your son," Bailey offered. "Perhaps his destiny is along the same path!"

"Could be!" I replied. "Of course, he also watches Kung Fu Panda three times a day, but it's probably too early to call him Bruce Lee."

Bailey flashed a smile that said she recognized my attempt at humor but had no idea who Bruce Lee was. I decided to put the kung fu talk aside to focus on project management instead.

"Bailey, it's always a pleasure for me to get to meet with our client managers. How can I help you?"

"The vice president of Marketing has a lot of interest in making sure this information database is implemented successfully," Bailey began. "He has given us the necessary time, but he has also made it very clear he doesn't want to hear excuses if it misses the deadline. I think Ashley is doing a good job, especially given the confusion that occurred when our old vice president was transferred. I guess I'm nervous because of the high visibility. We cannot afford to fail."

I acknowledged Bailey's nervousness. "That's a natural feeling, Bailey. In fact, you and Ashley are both on the hook for the success of this project. If there are problems, the VP is going to look to you for answers. It won't be good enough to say Ashley was the project manager and it was her responsibility."

"That's exactly my point," Bailey agreed, taking a deep breath. "The VP put me in charge of this project to make sure we hit our project budget and deadline. However, most of my background is in the finance area. I reviewed the business requirements document created by the project

team, but I don't have the expertise to evaluate the information. I want to be able to track the project adequately without getting involved in the details, but I don't know what questions to ask."

"It's hard for functional managers to be subject matter experts for every project in the organization," I said. "Your VP shouldn't expect you to have that level of knowledge. However, there are questions you can ask to make sure projects are progressing as expected. These questions are part of your quality assurance role."

LESSON

Managers want to delegate responsibility and autonomy to project managers, but they know they also retain a level of responsibility if the project is in trouble or fails. This accountability applies to the sponsor as well. Projects that fail or overrun their budgets and deadlines also reflect poorly on the sponsor and, to varying degrees, on all other management stakeholders.

So it's not surprising that a sponsor, functional manager, or other high-level manager wants to understand the status of a project. Of course, they can read status reports, but those are pretty much the project manager's viewpoint on status. In many cases, the status reports are so vague it is hard to know for sure what is going on.

So how do managers better understand the real status of a project? They could review the documentation being prepared, but most managers are not experts in the business aspects of all the projects in their organization. If the work involves an IT development project like Ashley's, they rarely have the expertise to understand the design documentation or the program code. Activities that focus on understanding the quality of deliverables are called *quality control*. Quality control is the responsibility of peers and specialists. Managers generally need to rely on *quality assurance* techniques instead.

Quality assurance does not focus on deliverable quality. Instead, quality assurance focuses on the processes that are used to build deliverables. If managers can't ensure that deliverables are of high quality based on their own experience, they must, at a minimum, feel that the project team used a solid process to build the deliverable.

In this instance, Bailey is in the project sponsor role, which was delegated to her by the vice president, who is the executive sponsor. Bailey is in the Marketing department, but her real expertise is in finance, and the executive sponsor named her as the project sponsor to ensure the project meets its budget and deadline commitments. It's not surprising that she is uncomfortable reviewing the business requirements document produced by the project team. Bailey can't look at the business requirements document and know for sure whether the requirements are correct and complete.

Fortunately, she doesn't have to. She should put on her quality assurance hat instead. What she really needs to know is how the requirements were created. To find out, she can ask some simple questions, such as the following:

- Who was involved in generating the requirements?
- Who reviewed the requirements?
- Who has approved the requirements so far?

Although she does not understand the detailed requirements herself, she should at least know a good process when she hears it. If she thinks the eliverable was created using a poor process, she can withhold her approval until a better process is followed. If she feels the process to create the requirements was sound, she should feel comfortable to approve the document. Here are some examples of poor processes and good processes.

Signs of a bad process:

- The requirements were generated by talking to only one or two people.
- No one has done a preliminary review of the content.
- The requirements were not approved by any of the people that provided requirements
- Key users were not involved in the requirements process.
- The document is sloppy, poorly formatted, and hard to read.

Signs of a good process:

- The requirements were generated by getting all the key users and stakeholders together in a facilitated session for a full day.
- Additional interested stakeholders from Legal, IT, and HR were consulted to understand how this project would impact their departments.
- The document has already been reviewed and approved by all major users and stakeholders.
- The document looks good, reads well, and follows a standard template format.

In this example, quality assurance was used to understand whether a specific deliverable was acceptable and should be approved by the sponsor. However, quality assurance is used on an ongoing basis by managers to understand the status of a project. The manager needs to ask questions regarding project management processes. This includes questions related to schedule, budget, issues, risk, quality, communication, etc. Quality assurance focuses on projects, and these are the processes used to manage a project.

Quality assurance is not a one-time activity. It should be an ongoing part of your project. The manager of the project manager and the sponsor are the key individuals who should be performing a quality assurance check at the end of every phase or during every major milestone.

If the project manager can explain and justify the process used to create the project deliverables, there is a good likelihood that the deliverables are acceptable. If the project is also using sound project management processes, the manager or sponsor performing the quality assurance check should have confidence that the project is on track.

Cancel Projects That Lose Business Support

"Hey, Tom! How are you doing? Everything going okay?" I didn't look up from my computer screen but immediately recognized Sam's voice. Sam Boyd, our Human Resources manager, was very "charismatic," to put it politely. It was mid-April and Sam was completing our company recruiting for spring college graduates.

"I am doing just fine; thanks for asking. How are things in Human Resources?"

"Everything is going great. I just finished an interview with a young man by the name of Ron Jobs, who will be graduating from Northeast Illinois State next month. I'm really impressed with him. He will graduate top of *his class and he seems sharp as a tack. I'd like to offer him a position here. Of course, I have to get an interview team set up...."*

"Did you say his last name was 'Jobs'?" I interrupted.

"Yes, but no relation to Steve. That was the first question I asked!"

"Don't blame you. I'm just checking to make sure your interest in him as a candidate isn't tainted by any desire for a new iPhone!"

Sam chuckled. Just then my phone rang. As a rule, the only time I interrupted a face-to-face discussion was when my boss was calling, but Sam motioned that he had to leave anyway, so I waved good-bye and picked up the call. I was surprised to find Emma Flood on the other end.

Emma was the IT director in our Chicago office and she wanted me to evaluate a project significantly over budget and long overdue to assess whether it is now on the right track. I agreed to offer my input and arranged to meet via teleconference later in the day with two of the major project participants.

My first meeting was with Curtis Chapman, the project manager. He was desperately trying to establish a revised schedule and budget. I asked him what the project sponsor thought of the revised schedule, and he said he had exchanged e-mails with her and she seemed happy that the project might finally be completed. I also asked whether the project charter had been updated. He insisted that there was really no need to update it since the original assumptions, deliverables, scope, etc. were the same as before.

Then I talked with Jennifer Adams, the project sponsor. Jennifer was very unhappy with the whole project and used the opportunity to vent her frustrations with the IT team. She held nothing back, saying it was doubtful the business value of the project would be achieved with the increased budget, and recent business changes made it questionable whether the original requirements were still valid. She said she would just be glad when the whole project was complete and behind her.

After the meetings, I collected my thoughts for a recommendation to Emma. When I spoke with her again, she was extremely curious as to what I thought of the project and its chance for future success.

I came right to the point. "Unless something changes very quickly, I think the project should be cancelled."

LESSON

One of the advantages of being the project adviser is that I normally don't have any attachment to the projects I evaluate. Ownership, or partial ownership, of a project can sometimes cloud one's ability to make rational decisions.

It is generally believed that if a project is approved, it must have inherent business value. In addition, the value must be such that the project is prioritized higher than other competing projects that are nominated but not approved. However, project business value can change as the project progresses. Market conditions change, project cost estimates change, and business priorities change. A project with great business value today might be irrelevant months, weeks, or even days later.

With that in mind, let's look at the project in the Chicago office. This project has already failed once, and is about to fail again. Sure, the project might be able to hit its revised timeline and budget—but what will the result be from a business perspective? The IT team, led by Curtis, is determined to deliver the project as it was originally defined, even if the assumptions and expectations of the client have changed considerably. Curtis wants to pretend everything is okay, even though he must realize the inherent problems with the initiative at this point. To be charitable, he may be hearing what he wants to hear from Jennifer, the project sponsor. He hears the sponsor saying she will be happy when the project is completed, but what she really wants is to get rid of the project. This is hardly the endorsement needed to proceed. The business situation has also changed, and the sponsor doubts the deliverables are even valid anymore.

Jennifer, the project sponsor, is not helping, either. In fact, she may be more at fault here, since she knows the project is probably a failure. The IT team could probably make the excuse that they were continuing the project because the sponsor never told them to stop. This is a poor excuse, but it might provide them with a bit of cover if the project implodes.

Jennifer, on the other hand, doesn't have any excuses. She is willing to spend additional company resources on an effort she has lost confidence in and from which she has already mentally checked out. She doubts the business value of the deliverables. She doesn't want to make the mental investment to try to revise the objectives or the scope to make the deliverables relevant again. Furthermore, the fact the sponsor is willing, even eager, to voice her displeasure with the project team is probably a sign the relationship between the sponsor and project manager has deteriorated beyond recovery.

Jennifer doesn't want to admit the work and money so far have been wasted. Since our company does not do a good job following up on whether projects achieve their business value, she probably feels the better alternative is to complete the project, gain some business value, and chalk the whole thing up to experience.

Both sides want to complete the project—but for the wrong reasons. The investment that has been made in this project may already be lost, and it appears that further investment in the project in its current form would be throwing even more good money away. After I make my report to Emma, she might be in a position to recommend that the project business case be re-evaluated. It's possible the project could continue with new sponsorship and a new project manager, but it would then probably need to restart with the planning process to make sure it is still delivering something of value to the new sponsor.

There is a lot working against this project. For now, the project should be placed on hold or simply cancelled. Sometimes it's better not to complete a project. This is one of those times.

Use Risk Management to Discover Potential Problems

I received an e-mail from Jade Johnson on April 30 asking if she could come by and see me. Jade's team was making a number of changes to the interface files going to and coming from our main bank. I told her she could come by in the afternoon. She was a little vague and explained that her problem was not yet "official," but she would contact me in a few days. I wasn't sure what she meant, but she said she would explain later.

Jade called me a week later to schedule an afternoon meeting, and I had to admit she had aroused my curiosity. She arrived five minutes early for our appointment, and since I was already in my office, I asked her to come in.

"How are you today, Jade?"

"I'm fine, Tom. How are you?"

"Things are great; thanks for asking. Tell me, though, Jade, what's going on with your project? You mentioned last week you had a problem, but it was not an 'official' problem. Can I assume it is now?"

"Sorry for the confusion, Tom. Yes, it is a problem now. You see, last week I was speaking to one of our team members and she told me Kristen in the Finance department is pregnant! She then told me it was a secret for now and I shouldn't mention it to anyone. Of course, this causes a big problem for us, but I could not address it until she officially announced it. I got an e-mail from Kristen this morning letting me know about her pregnancy, so now I guess the cat's out of the bag."

Jade explained how many of the activities in the project plan relied on Kristen's expertise; she was going to be instrumental in the success of the project since she provided the business expertise and leadership for setting up the bank interfaces a few years ago. Jade wanted to rely on Kristen again, but Kristen's e-mail mentioned she was three months pregnant and would be taking an extended leave from work after the baby was born.

"Here is my dilemma," Jade said. "If we're lucky, we will have the project done by the time Kristen has her baby. But if the baby comes early or if the project is delayed, we could be in trouble."

I asked Jade how she planned to account for this.

"Well, I called you just to be sure," she said. "I think this is definitely an issue. And you know what you always say—'issues are big problems.'"

I laughed. "I guess I should look into trademarking that saying if it is so easily quoted! In this situation, though, the issue is not yet a problem. It is a potential problem. You should identify it and manage it as a project risk."

LESSON

Issues and risks are related but not the same. Issues are large problems present today that will impede the project if left unresolved. They must be focused on and resolved quickly. You have no other choice. By its nature, issues management is a reactive project management process, since you do not invoke it until the issue has already arisen.

On the other hand, risks are future conditions or circumstances outside the control of the project team that will have an adverse impact on the project should they occur. (There is a concept of positive risk but that is a topic for another lesson.) In other words, an issue is a current problem that must be dealt with, whereas a risk is a potential future problem. The good thing about a risk is you have some time to deal with the potential problem. Risk management is the process of identifying, analyzing, responding to, and controlling project risks. Risk management is a proactive project management process, since you are trying to deal with potential future events before they occur.

Risk management is not a one-time process. You should always identify risks at the beginning of the project during the up-front planning process, but you should also periodically look at remaining work to identify any new risks. This evaluation can take place on a periodic basis (e.g., monthly) or at project milestones.

Such is the case with Jade's project. When the project started, there was no mention of the risk associated with losing Kristen, the strongest and most experienced analyst in the client organization. This makes sense. Although there is a very small chance any individual person might leave a project team, there is no reason to elevate this to a risk needing to be identified and managed.

However, circumstances have changed, and now there is a definite possibility that Kristen will not be available before the project is completed. Kristen is still on the project today, so there is no issue to be dealt with immediately. There is, however, a potential problem in the future. It is possible that the project will be over before Kristen leaves or past a point where Kristen's expertise is critical. However, this result can't be taken for granted, hence the need to identify this as a project risk.

Identifying this as a risk is the first step. Next is to analyze the risk to see if it is important enough to manage. If it is, a risk plan must be created to respond to the risk. In this case, Jade must put a risk plan in place to respond to this potential problem. A common objective of the risk plan is mitigation, which means you try to minimize the probability of the risk occurring and/or minimize the impact to the project if the risk occurs. (There are other risk response options, which will be explained in another lesson). Looking at Jade's project, the timing of the new baby's arrival can't be controlled, so eliminating the risk event is not an option. However, since Jade has identified this risk early, she has plenty of time to minimize the impact of the event to ensure the project can still be completed successfully. Potential options for Jade to consider include:

- Accelerating the work Kristen needs to perform so there is a higher likelihood it will be completed before she leaves. This could still be risky since she may have to leave early.
- Cross-training a replacement who can take over from Kristen if she has to leave early.
- Replacing Kristen with another resource, while still utilizing her as a backup and a mentor for her replacement (if this fits with the Human Resources policies).

Since Jade has time, this project risk will likely be resolved before there is an impact on the project. That is the nature of risks. Since they are future events, you have some time to minimize them or prepare for them before they occur.

Focus Quality Management on Processes, Not People

Jerry called me to set up an afternoon meeting on May 1. I invited him to lunch, but he asked for a rain check as his schedule was crazy. Jerry and I exchanged e-mails frequently, so I knew that he and his wife were getting excited about moving into Wayne's house. The Morettis were moving to Arizona in July and planned to leave Illinois during the last week of June. Jerry was already beginning to pack up the apartment, preparing to move in shortly after the Morettis moved out. Jerry had filled out the necessary paperwork to take over ownership of the Morettis' home and had already secured the mortgage from the bank. I volunteered to help him move when the time came and he gladly accepted.

Jerry was also approaching a significant milestone at Mega Manufacturing—or at least I thought it was significant. He was in the final week or two of his project to upgrade the phone mail system, and most of the changes had already been implemented. He had not had a major problem pop up for almost a month, and I could tell his confidence was sky-high as he witnessed the fruits of his labor. At least it was sky-high before last Friday.

Jerry arrived on time for our meeting and began filling me in on the problem he had encountered. He was wearing a blue suit with a red-and-yellow-striped tie.

"Why the fancy suit, Jerry? Do you have a job interview today?" I joked.

"No, actually Barbara and I are celebrating our anniversary today. I am taking her to a pricey restaurant for dinner right after work."

"That's great. Happy anniversary!" I said, standing up to shake his hand. "Sounds like buying the Moretti's house was perfectly timed. Makes for a great anniversary gift!"

"We are definitely excited about that, to be sure. Still, though, doesn't get me out of the fancy dinner!"

I smiled knowingly. Jerry filled me in on his dinner plans before getting down to business.

"The CIO asked us to give him a demo of the new voicemail software," he started. "This should not have been a problem, but when we went to his office, wouldn't you know it—the system didn't work right! We had to come back half an hour later to finish the demonstration. He liked the new system, but I'm not sure he is totally confident in our ability to install it."

"Sounds embarrassing," I said. "What went wrong?"

"We're trying to get additional people trained on how to install the software," he replied. "Unfortunately, we assigned one of our newer people to work on the CIO setup, and he missed one of the steps. Maybe he can't be trusted to do the upgrade. We may have to remove him from the project."

"Whoa," I cautioned. "You have thousands of phones to upgrade. I think you are going to need all the help you can get. Tell me, what procedures are in place to help these new technicians?"

Jerry thought carefully for a minute. "The techs are supposed to under-stand the phones and the voicemail software. We spent time showing each person what needs to be done for the upgrade, and we assume they are skilled enough and professional enough to do the job."

I started to see a problem with the team's quality process. "You know, you are going to have to upgrade dozens of phone switches and thou-sands of phones for this project. It seems to me that even if your team is very diligent, there is a good chance problems will crop up on some of the installations. High-quality projects are only partially the result of good people. They are also the result of having good quality processes. When quality problems like this surface, don't blame your people—fix your processes instead."

LESSON

If people always produced high-quality results, there would be no need for quality management. However, even the best people make mistakes, includ-ing project managers! Sometimes they don't even know it. For instance, quality problems can result from simple misunderstandings. You may be doing everything right as far as you know, and problems can still occur.

One core project management responsibility is to manage the overall quality of the deliverables produced. Creating a quality plan that identifies quality control activities and quality assurance activities is one aspect of managing the overall quality.

Quality control activities validate the specific quality of the deliverables. It is also referred to as *inspection*. For instance, a peer review of engineering de-sign specs is a quality control activity.

Quality assurance activities focus on the processes used to create the deliver-ables. This is also called *prevention*. The thought is that if you have good processes, you will build good deliverables. Quality assurance could include a quality audit to ensure all aspects of a manufacturing process were followed.

A project team can't deliver consistent, high-quality products without good processes in place. Of course, you want to have good, motivated people as well. But if you put good people into a complex, chaotic situation without good processes or guidelines, they are bound to struggle.

Quality processes must be scaled to the size, complexity, and importance of the project. Small projects should have simple, basic quality checks built into the schedule. Larger projects should have good overall quality processes in place, as well as metrics to determine the level of quality being produced. The team should monitor the quality metrics and improve the overall work processes when possible.

Note that nothing described so far focuses on people. There is no mention of hiring only the best people or reassigning people who make mistakes. If good processes are in place, and if people work according to those processes, then everything should be fine. In a quality-focused organization, you don't blame people when things go wrong. People are bound to make mistakes. It's human nature. When mistakes occur, you make process changes to prevent the errors from occurring in the future.

Let's go back and look at Jerry's project. Jerry's frustration with a team member's performance is misplaced. Sure, it hurt when the upgrade process failed for the CIO. But other employees are bound to face similar problems as the upgrade is rolled out. What is he going to do—replace every team member who makes a mistake? Instead, Jerry needs to focus on processes. Right now Jerry is asking his team members to perform their work with very little structure and support, while he hopes nothing will go wrong. That's not a recipe for success.

Instead, he should create a quality process to ensure everyone will be successful. This process could include activities such as providing better initial training, creating written procedures or checklists, pairing up new members with more experienced people, and having a second person perform quick random checks of the phones as they are converted. Quality-focused organizations (and projects) realize that prevention is the first choice of action over inspection—although they are both important. Prevention (QA) helps ensure good processes are in place to prevent errors. Inspection (QC) ensures that any remaining errors are caught. Jerry needs a Quality Plan with both aspects in place to ensure his project progresses with as high a level of quality as possible.

Don't Use Your Estimating Contingency for Scope Changes

May 5 was a fun day for the employees at Mega Manufacturing. The company always paid for a nice Cinco de Mayo luncheon from Tico Taco, one of the few Mexican restaurants in Dickens. For most people, the annual party provided a nice opportunity to get outside and enjoy socializing with colleagues in an open environment. It was always fun to see Dennis Lucas, our CEO, wearing a sombrero. Dennis was in his 60s and wore small, round glasses on his tiny head. He was also bald, which allowed the sombrero to slide over his ears to the top of his glasses—always an entertaining sight to see.

I was enjoying a burrito with extra jalapeños when Jeff Erickson came over to say hello. Jeff had just returned from a week's vacation in the Bahamas, which he won from a radio station after correctly identifying a montage of songs from the 1980s. He had a dark tan and a bright smile on his face.

"I take it the vacation went well," I said as I shook his hand.

"It was incredible, Tom, and so relaxing. My wife and I tanned on the beach every day and just listened to the waves crashing as we sipped piña coladas. I feel like a new man!"

Jeff and I worked a lot together when I was still with the IT department, but I had not spoken to him since the New Year's Eve party. He was a tall guy with a big body frame. He liked to lift weights and frequently worked out at the gym during his lunch hour. He was not the typical computer nerd, which is probably why we got along so well when we worked together.

"Say, Tom, I wonder if I could ask your opinion on a problem I am having with a project?"

"Sure Jeff. What's going on?"

Jeff gave me a quick summary of his project involving the installation of manufacturing software for one of his clients. He spoke about his project charter and the progress his team had made so far. He also mentioned it was the fourth time he had installed this software at one of our plants.

"The installation process for this software is similar at each plant, but each plant has its own unique needs. For instance, the plant manager in our current installation has requested we implement a custom inventory management module the other plants don't need."

"A custom module?" I asked in surprise. "I thought you said you were only going to implement base package functionality. If there is a new business need, I hope you are invoking scope change management."

"I talked to the client about scope change," he replied. "But he knows our cost estimate includes a 15 percent contingency. He approved the additional contingency, so he thought we could use that funding for this new work."

"Tell me, why did you include the 15 percent estimating contingency?"

"The contingency covers a couple of unknowns," Jeff explained. "I am the only one on the team who has done this kind of project before and it may take some time to get the rest of my team up to speed. We are also installing a newer release of the package than was installed at the other plants. The other packages are all an older release."

"Those sound like valid reasons to add contingency," I concluded. "What will happen if your people need extra time with the learning curve or the new software has some unexpected glitches, but you have used up your contingency on work outside of scope?"

Jeff was getting the idea. "I guess the project will be over budget. Then I will look like a bad project manager, even though I thought I was being client focused."

LESSON

The only time you know for sure what a project will cost and how long it will take is after the work is completed. By its very nature, estimating is a guess. Of course, by using proper estimating techniques, you can make it a very close guess. However, there is always some degree of uncertainty in an estimate.

One of the steps in the estimating process is to add contingency to reflect the level of uncertainty associated with the estimate. If your estimate is at a high level, the contingency could be plus or minus 50 percent or more. However, even if most of the facts are known, a contingency of plus or minus 15 percent is not unreasonable. This contingency can apply to effort, cost, and schedule.

When you place a contingency in the project, everyone should understand it is there to absorb the estimating uncertainty. However, once the estimate is approved, there may be pressure to use the contingency budget for additional and/or new requirements instead. Your client may start to think of the contingency as "extra money" to be spent as needed. Although it is tempting to use the contingency when new functionality is requested, the project manager must ensure the estimating contingency is used as intended.

Jeff's project has just begun, and there is already a request to use the contingency. Using the contingency for this additional requirement would open the project up to two risks. First, the project could go over budget if the uncertainties associated with the original estimate come true. The budget contingency is there in case activities cost more than estimated. If you use the contingency for scope change requests, you will have less left over for true estimating errors. As Jeff realizes, he will then be seen as a poor manager (or a poor estimator) even though he thinks he is being client focused by agreeing to his client's request.

Second, by skipping the change process, Jeff is denying the sponsor an opportunity to make a decision as to whether the requested change is justified from a cost/benefit perspective. Instead, he and the plant manager are making the decision themselves. Although the plant manager is a key stakeholder, he is not the person funding this project. He is not the decision maker for scope change requests.

Jeff's best option now is to push the request through the scope change process and let the sponsor determine if it is worth the incremental time and cost to the project. If so, the project budget and timeline should be increased to cover the work.

The client should not worry that the contingency budget will be wasted. As the project progresses, portions of the estimating contingency can be released back to the client if the project is trending on or ahead of budget. Any money remaining from the estimating contingency budget at the end of the project can be returned to the organization.

Develop a Communication Plan for Complex Projects

The burritos, tortilla chips, and guacamole were creating a heavy feeling in my stomach, so I decided to skip the remainder of the party and take a walk. There was a small wine shop about a block south of the Mega Manufacturing building, and I thought a quick walk there and back would do me good. Of course, one can't just walk to a wine shop without taking a quick look around, so I factored a quick stop into my schedule. I figured I could make it there and back in 30 minutes, which would coincide nicely with the end of the Cinco de Mayo party.

The Wine Depot was owned by Brent Bonds, and it carried a nice variety of everyday wines as well as a few hard-to-find gems. Brent was very knowledgeable and always made good recommendations. A tiny bell atop the door rang as I entered, and Brent poked his head over the top row of bottles in the Merlot section to say hello.

I browsed among the wines on display in the store for a few minutes and decided to buy a bottle of Columbia Crest Grand Estates Chardonnay on sale for $11.99. Pam was making fish for dinner and Brent said the chardonnay would go perfectly with the meal.

"Is this wine going to taste like a tree or like a stick of butter?" I said jokingly.

"Hopefully it will taste like crushed grapes," Brent said, returning my sarcasm.

"Good one. I'll let you know how it tasted." Brent and I exchanged a few more kind words before I headed back to the office.

I was surprised to find Reyna Andersen waiting outside my door. She explained she had just come from a meeting with her sponsor. Going into the meeting, she was working on a straightforward project to implement a customer relationship management (CRM) package. After the meeting, however, the project had become much more complex, and she wanted to talk to me about it immediately. I tucked my bottle of wine into my bag and asked Reyna to come in and sit down.

"My sponsor just informed me that her division has reorganized," she began. "We need to implement this CRM package in our Canadian and Mexican operations as well."

"Wow, that's a major change!" I replied. "I bet you want to talk to me about change management."

"Actually, I don't," she replied. "I explained to the sponsor her request was way outside the scope we agreed to. She agreed and asked us to come up with a new estimated budget and end date. My biggest concern is being able to communicate and work successfully in the other countries. I have never been to either country, and I don't know what to expect."

"I think I would have the same concerns," I agreed. "There are no specific problems right now, but when you are working internationally, communication cannot be taken for granted. The good news is the change in scope has come before the project has gone too far. You should have time to deal with it."

"Exactly!" Reyna replied. "But I don't know what to do next. This CRM initiative requires a culture change for the sales staff. Communication was already critical, and now it is even more so. I need to call a team meeting to try to get a handle on the communication needs and work with my team to plan how we can successfully operate in these different cultures."

"Bingo!" I said approvingly. "You have solved your own problem."

LESSON

Culture has been described as "how we do things 'round here." Culture change refers to changing the way people perform their jobs. In other words, you are changing how people "do things 'round here." Implementing a culture change initiative in an organization requires a multifaceted communication strategy to be successful.

The potential problems associated with a culture change project can usually be managed with a Change Management Plan. The key element of a Culture Change Plan will be a multifaceted Communication Plan. Creating a Communication Plan involves following a simple process.

- Identify the key clients, users, stakeholders, etc.
- Determine their communication needs.
- Brainstorm ways to fulfill the communication needs. This is an opportunity to be creative.
- Evaluate the options in step 3 to determine which provide the most value at the least cost and impact to the project—and cover all of the stakeholders to some degree. Since you can't do everything, these are the communication activities to start with.
- Fill in the communication activity details and move to the project schedule. This includes who is assigned to the communication activity, the timing of the communication, the effort required, any dependencies, etc.

Step 3 is the time to be creative about how you fulfill the communication needs. You will need more than just status reports. You will need a multi-faceted and holistic set of communication activities. Think about communication options in the following three main categories.

- **Mandatory**: This generally includes project status reports, legal requirements, financial reporting, etc. This information is pushed out to the recipients.
- **Informational**: This includes information people want to know or information that the project team wants to provide for them. This information is usually made available for people to read but requires them to take the initiative or *pull* the communication. An example is having a project website.
- **Marketing**: These activities help to build buy-in and enthusiasm for the project and its deliverables (if you can't build enthusiasm, at least keep people neutral). This communication is pushed out to the appropriate people. Examples include newsletters, success stories, project posters, milestone celebrations, speaking at department meetings, etc.

Even though Reyna has not had responsibility for an international project, others in the company have. She needs to speak to them to determine the type of communication and interaction that works best with the Canadian and Mexican staff. Once she has a good Communication Plan in place, she should monitor it to ensure people are getting the information they need. If not, the plan should be modified as appropriate during the project. This could mean modifying current communication activities, eliminating ineffective activities, or coming up with new communication ideas based on the experience of the project so far.

Good proactive communication is vital in a culture change initiative like this. It is not the only area Reyna must address, but it is the foundation upon which all other culture change activities will be built.

Scale Your Processes Based on Project Size

Sam in Human Resources set up a meeting with me for the afternoon of May 28 with a new employee. It was Ron Jobs, the recent graduate Sam mentioned to me last month. He had accepted our offer and had been on the job for about a week. The two of them came by my office around 2 p.m. and Sam introduced us.

"Tom Mochal, this is Ron Jobs," he said. "Ron just graduated from Northeast Illinois State and started with us last week." Ron looked young. I wondered if I looked that young when I graduated college. He was 22 or 23, and his overall look was crisp and professional. I didn't know how smart or skilled he was, but he looked like a businessman. I was impressed.

"It's a pleasure meeting you," I replied. "Actually, I remember Sam speaking briefly about you after your initial company interviews. If I remember correctly, you were top of your class."

"That's right," Ron said with pride. "I am really anxious to get started and prove myself."

"That's actually why I brought Ron by today," Sam interjected. "He is starting a new project and I want you to give him some advice on how best to proceed."

Surprisingly, Sam said little else and left shortly thereafter, giving Ron and me some time to discuss his assignment. He was responsible for creating a real-time equipment utilization report for a manufacturing division client. Actually, I was a little concerned. It was not unusual to give new people responsibility, but to ask Ron to lead a project as his first assignment seemed aggressive. Perhaps he had some prior experience managing projects at school.

"Tom," Ron began, "I know you have a standard project charter document and I want some help developing it for the first time. I have a good idea what the objectives and scope are, but I'm not sure about a couple of the other sections like risk, budget, and the overall approach."

"Great," I replied. "We can walk through the major risks, and I can also give you a risk template for you to complete on your own."

"Good. I am also not sure exactly how we do budgeting here, so I will need some help going over my estimate and determining what the cost will be."

The kid sure seemed to be asking the right questions. "Not a problem. I can give you an overview of how we do budgeting, and then you can confirm some of the details with your manager."

"I think the only other area I am not sure about is the project approach section. I just need more clarity on what you expect to see there."

"That section can be a little tricky, but by the time you get your initial schedule laid out, you should have the information you need to complete the approach. How many people will be working with you on this project?"

Ron was a little surprised. "Well, right now I am the only one identified," he said.

Now it was my turn to be surprised. "Really? You are going to put the whole application together yourself?"

"Yes. There will just be one new online screen to create," Ron said.

I was beginning to get the picture. "Ron, how much effort are you estimating it will take to complete this work?"

"I should be able to complete it in about 40 hours," Ron said.

I was able to shift gears and start down a new line of questioning. The rest of our conversation focused on gathering only the information Ron needed to define a small enhancement project.

LESSON

Much of the work done in a company can be structured and organized as a project. In turn, all projects need to be managed. However, the process (or methodology) used to manage the work needs to scale up and down, depending on the size of the work effort.

For instance, large projects should have a formal definition and planning phase, as well as rigorous processes for managing and controlling the work. In fact, it is not unusual for a very large project of 10,000 hours to require 1,500 hours of project management time. Medium-sized projects still require some level of planning and some processes for managing and controlling the work. For instance, on a 1,000-hour project, only 150 hours of project management time might be needed. Note that the percentage is the same (15 percent), but the total hours are down considerably. The same rigorous project management processes for a 10,000-hour project would not be needed for a 1,000-hour project.

How about a small project? A person may not need much formal planning or managing at all if the project is small enough. The planning and managing could probably be done in the person's head as he goes. For instance, a 10-hour project may only need an hour of project management. This hour is not spent on formal project management procedures, but it might include completing a simple work authorization form, mapping a plan of attack in your head, and some simple communication with stakeholders.

Let's look again at Ron's project. I give him credit for being eager to follow project management processes, but he is not scaling the processes appropriately. It doesn't make sense to spend 10 hours to write a project charter for a project requiring only 40 hours of effort. He doesn't need to define formal objectives, scope, or approach. Those concepts have less meaning for small work efforts. The chances of running into a major change or having to manage a risk are very small on a project of this size. Even if he does, what would be the consequences? Perhaps his 40-hour project will end up taking 60 hours. This is 50 percent over its original estimate, but it is not going to bankrupt the company. Projects of this size do not need formal project management processes.

Fortunately, our department has some processes and forms that reinforce the scalable nature of the work. For instance, we have a one-page document called a Service Request Form that is used to define small enhancements and other minor initiatives. Once I realized the work effort was small, I made Ron aware of this form and we spent the rest of our meeting going over the handful of items on it. All projects should be documented and approved— even small ones. The Service Request Form allows the client manager to see the request and the estimated effort. The client manager can then approve the service request as well as prioritize the work against all of the other service requests that might be under consideration at any given time.

The lesson for Ron is to make sure he does not blindly follow a methodology. Our organization has some standards for all projects, and of course these should be followed. However, after the mandatory standards, the rest of the project management process should be scaled based on the size of the project.

Plan the Project Even If You Start the Work at the Same Time

Brian White was a project manager in his early 30s who had a reputation for being very easygoing and extremely well liked. A talented musician, he often played his guitar around town at open microphone nights in bars or coffee shops. He put up fliers in the break rooms advertising these events, and there were always at least a few employees who showed up to cheer him on. I had never seen him perform, but I heard he played a mellow set, including several cover songs from Simon and

Garfunkel. Given his relatively young age, I was surprised to find out about his affinity for the "Bridge over Troubled Water" duo. A few weeks ago, I helped Brian put together an estimate for a wireless Internet project for Mega Manufacturing's R&D department. He had good news and bad news when I met with him for the second time.

"The estimate we worked on a few weeks ago has been accepted!" he said, smiling broadly. "However, the timeline for completing the project has been shortened. My manager said a couple of other business units are interested in the new technology, and they want this proof-of-concept project completed as soon as possible."

"Well, I guess that's good news," I agreed. "Do you need help with the project charter? I think the project is small enough that we can use the abbreviated version."

"I agree the definition document is normally important," Brian said. "But we are already past the planning process. Based on this earlier deadline date, we are already starting the work."

I could foresee potential problems if Brian went forward like this. "Really?" I questioned. "What are your deliverables? What is your approach? Where is your timeline? What is in scope and out of scope?"

Brian could only give me partial answers, which made me even more nervous. The shortened deadline was making him think he didn't have time for planning.

"It sounds like you only have a vague idea of what you are going to do and what the expectations are," I pointed out. "One of the purposes of definition and planning is to ensure you have an agreement with your sponsor on what is expected. Otherwise, you will only be able to define your plans and deliverables after you have started the project—and by then it will be too late to meet your deadline.

"But what about that deadline?" Brian insisted. "We've got to start now if we want to get the work done on time."

"Planning is not a luxury you do only if you have time," I countered. "Planning is part of the project. If you have a choice, it's better to define and plan the project first, and then execute the plan. However, sometimes you have to start the project immediately and plan the work while some of it is already in progress."

LESSON

Project managers often need to start working on a project before the planning is complete. This can be because of time pressure, like Brian's project, or it can be caused by the project team being assigned before the planning is complete. In the latter case, the project manager needs to have work available to keep the team members busy even though planning is not complete. This is not an optimal situation, but it happens all the time.

When project execution starts early, there is a tendency to think you can get by without the upfront definition and planning. However, this is not the case. If you don't plan, you won't know what your deliverables are, what your scope is, or what the schedule looks like. Even if you think you know the answers, you will not have confirmed that they are correct with your sponsor to make sure you are all on the same page.

It is possible to successfully plan the project after the execution work has started. The trick is to assign resources to activities you are confident will need to be done in any case. For instance, most projects have some upfront analysis work. You can assign resources to work on the analysis while you are completing the planning. The ability to assign and manage work—while also performing the initial planning—is time consuming and requires the project manager to be well organized, disciplined, and able to multitask. Some people say it is like changing the tires on a moving vehicle. It's hard work, which is another reason why many project managers skip it if the project has already started.

At some point, the definition and planning work will be completed. The project manager now has an agreement with the sponsor on the work that needs to be done and a schedule that shows how to get it done. The project manager can then confirm the work completed so far and can make sure nothing critical has been missed. You may have assigned and completed some unnecessary work, but that is the tradeoff for having to start the work early. Hopefully, any wasted work effort will be made up for by an increased ability to deliver to an early deadline. On a project like this, the deadline date is normally more important than the effort and cost, and your sponsor is usually willing to be a little inefficient to achieve the deadline date.

The reward of this definition and planning is the ability to manage the rest of the project proactively.

What happens if you don't finish the planning work? The alternative scenario is that the project execution work gets too far ahead and the planning process never catches up. If you skip the definition and planning process, the risks to the project include the following:

- An inaccurate schedule, resulting in missed activities or extra, unnecessary activities throughout the project.
- A loose understanding of scope, resulting in a large number of scope changes.
- Deliverables that do not meet the client's expectations.
- Uncertainty of the project risks and how to respond to them.

In this specific project, I don't recommend that Brian stop everything to complete the definition and the planning process. However, he still needs to proceed with the planning while the project is executing. In the short term, he can identify work that must be done, regardless of the outcome of the planning process, and assign team members to this work. Brian should also get formal approval of the Project Charter. Based on the size of his project, he can define the work by completing an Abbreviated Project Charter. When the Abbreviated Project Charter and schedule are complete, he can synchronize the plan with the work already done and proactively manage the rest of the project from there.

Identify the Critical Path and How This Path Drives the End Date

The majority of my work involved meeting with people and helping them through one or two particular project problems. I rarely had a chance to meet with someone regularly and help them complete their project from start to finish. That was a big reason why Jerry and I had become very comfortable working with each other. Meeting with him regularly made me feel like a part of the team and allowed me to see not only the progression of the project but also his professional progression as he learned more and more about being a better project manager.

Another person I helped frequently—although not as often as Jerry—was Ashley Parker. It was the middle of June; her team had just completed work on the new marketing information database, and she had invited me to attend their project conclusion meeting. The project finished three weeks behind schedule and was over budget by 15 percent—not terrible numbers, but an interesting discussion ensued as to the cause of these overruns and how they could have been avoided. Ashley began the meeting by congratulating the team on a job well done.

"First off, my sincerest thanks to all of you for working so hard on this project. You all did a wonderful job, and you should feel proud of your work and our accomplishment. Of course, as with any project, we did encounter a few problems. That's the purpose for our meeting this morning. Knowing what we know today, what could we have done differently on the project to hit our deadline and budget?"

Chris, one of the database administrators, spoke up. "For the first half of the project, everything seemed to go according to schedule. But some of the design decisions we made up front didn't pan out like we hoped and caused us rework delays later on."

"That's a good point," Ashley noted. "The design work is critical on a project deploying new technology. For a project like this, that type of work should have been on the critical path."

"I think we also lost some focus toward the middle of the project," Diane contributed. "As we started to create the physical database, we were heading into the holiday season. I think things started to slip at that point."

"You're right," Ashley agreed, nodding. "It's imperative to maintain work focus around the holidays. If I had to do it again, I would have added some of those activities to the critical path as well."

"Another thing I noticed," Ashley continued diplomatically, "was I had problems understanding some aspects of the project management tool we were using. About halfway through the project, I was looking at the project's critical path. The tool was cluttering the critical path with lots of unimportant activities. Other longer and more important activities were not on the path. Next time I run a project, I am going to move the *more important activities onto the critical path, so I can place the proper amount of management focus on them."*

I decided at this point to put on my coach's hat. The discussion on key learning from the project was a good one, but I didn't want them to encounter other problems on their next project because of faulty understanding of the critical path.

LESSON

Before I discuss the critical path, I'll clarify the definition of *schedule float*. *Float*, or *slack*, refers to a time lag that can occur between two activities without impacting the final deadline. For instance, let's say you have two activities—A and B. Activity B must start after activity A has finished. If activity B must start right away, there is zero slack. However, if activity B can start two days after activity A finishes without impacting the overall deadline date, then activity B has two days of slack. This does not mean activity B must wait two days. However, if necessary, activity B could wait up to two days without impacting the overall project deadline.

With that in mind, let's look at the critical path. *Critical path* is the name given to the sequence of activities from start to finish that must be started and completed on time for the entire project to complete on time. There is no float for any activity on the path. Every project has a critical path of activities, and the project end date is based on the length of time to complete the tasks on the critical path.

For example, imagine a project takes 300 days. The critical path might consist of a sequence of 40 activities that would also take 300 days to complete. If the first activity on the critical path is 1 day late, the project will take 301 days to complete, unless another activity on the critical path can be completed 1 day earlier.

It is vital the project manager understands the critical path and pays special attention to these activities, since any delay on the critical path will result in a delay in the entire project. If your project is behind schedule, you must accelerate activities on the critical path to get back on schedule. If the project is behind schedule and the project manager is not aware of the critical path and how it drives the project end date, it's likely that precious resources will be misapplied on the wrong activities.

There are two common misconceptions about the critical path. The first is that all of the activities on the path are important, or critical. However, this is not necessarily the case. While some activities on the path can be very important, it is also likely that many mundane activities are there as well. The activities on the critical path are critical from a scheduling perspective since they drive the end date, but they may or may not be of critical importance to the project.

The second misconception is the project manager can add critical, or important, activities to the critical path. This is what I am hearing from Ashley at her end-of-project meeting. She would like to have all her critical (important) activities added to the critical path because she perceives she will spend more time focusing on the activities there. She is right about the additional scrutiny, but she has a basic misconception about how the critical path is calculated and how the activities get there.

That's when I step in to explain the critical path to Ashley and the others. The critical path is what it is from a scheduling perspective, and the project manager can't add activities to it just because those activities are important. In fact, if new activities are forced onto the critical path, the result will be a delay on the project. For instance, if you arbitrarily force a 10-day activity onto your 300-day project, the result would be that the project takes 310 days to complete. That's not what you want.

I compliment Ashley on her desire to place more focus on certain activities, but ask her to determine the most important activities and place the appropriate level of focus on those—regardless of whether they are on the critical path or not.

Change Assumptions to Revise an Estimate

Working with Jerry for the last six months had been a real treat for me. When Jerry first started his project to update the phone mail system, he was inexperienced and had no idea how to approach project management in an efficient and organized fashion. Now he was much more knowledgeable. He wasn't a seasoned pro by any means, but he had come a long way in a short time. We celebrated the completion of his project to upgrade the phone system and software a few weeks ago, and so far, there had been very few complaints—and an abundance of compliments on a job well done.

In fact, Jerry did such a good job on the phone project he was given another big assignment: deploying an operating system upgrade on all

Mega Manufacturing desktops. It was a large project and involved more team members and more responsibility, but Jerry's confidence was high and I could tell he felt capable of handling the job. His confidence was noteworthy, especially given where he was just a few months ago. It was also significant considering he and his wife would be moving into the Morettis' house in a few weeks. Clearly the organizational skills and confidence gained at work were carrying over into his personal life because he showed no signs of stress or worry about the move.

Jerry came to see me at the end of June to discuss feedback he had received from his manager on the desktop upgrade project. Jerry's manager had just read his draft project charter. Apparently, he liked the overall definition and plan but had a problem with the cost estimate.

"Are you ready for your big move, Jerry?" I asked as he entered the office.

"We sure are, Tom. Barbara already has a list of things she wants to change after we move in. We are both really excited."

"Are you planning any major changes?"

"Not at all. Barb wants to do some painting in certain rooms to better match our color schemes, and we are thinking about changing the tile in the master bathroom. Small things, really."

"Sounds good. As always, let me know how I can help. So tell me, where are things with your project?"

"Well, I'm not sure what to do next," Jerry began. "I worked with a number of technical experts to prepare the effort and cost estimate for this project, but my manager says it's too high."

"Did your manager give you any insight as to why he thought the estimate was too high?" I asked.

"As best I can tell, the estimate is too high because it's more than the budget allocated for this work," Jerry explained. "He said if the numbers were closer to budget, he would just go ahead, but my estimate is 60 percent more than the initial budget allocation."

"Really?" I asked. "Well, the original budget was proposed last year during the business planning process. Those numbers are put forward at a pretty high level. It is not surprising your more detailed estimate is much

higher. It's also probably much more accurate. Did your boss have any advice on how to reduce the number?"

"Not really," he replied. *"He just said he wanted me to 'sharpen my pencil' some more and try to get the project estimate down substantially. This really stinks!"*

"Hang in there," I said encouragingly. *"You should not be forced into making an estimate you don't believe in. However, let's look at some options that might help you out."*

LESSON

Jerry is not the first person to have an estimate questioned, and he will not be the last. This scenario happens all the time. The project to upgrade the desktop operating system was proposed and approved last year as part of the business planning process. The company also allocated a preliminary budget to the work. However, managers don't have the time to perform a detailed effort and cost estimate for each project during the yearly planning process. Those budgets are estimated at a high level and need to be validated once the actual project starts.

That's where we are now. Jerry was assigned to the project and is defining and planning the work at a lower level of detail. As a result, Jerry has created a much more realistic estimate of the costs involved, and his new figures are 60 percent higher than the original budget. The company expects the estimates to be off somewhat. In fact, Jerry's boss told him if his estimate was closer to the original budget, they could go back and ask for more money. However, his boss feels he will not be able to ask for a 60 percent increase. That type of increase will either not be funded at all, or the additional funding will probably require another approved project to be cancelled.

This puts Jerry in a tough position. The company wants to do the work—that's why it was approved for this year. However, now they may not be able to afford it. Jerry's boss wants the estimate reduced and has asked Jerry to "sharpen his pencil." On the surface, Jerry's manager is asking him to make the estimate more accurate. However, the clear implication is he wants the estimate reduced. His boss is assuming Jerry's estimate is sloppy or has some inherent padding that can be removed.

Jerry's first thought is that he needs to reduce the estimate arbitrarily and then take the heat when the work comes in over budget. That is definitely not the path to take. Instead, he should look at two areas.

First, Jerry needs to verify his own estimate. If he used an estimating tool or a spreadsheet, he should double-check the formulas, confirm that he is using the right resource rates, and make sure the non-labor costs are reasonably accurate. Once he is convinced his math is accurate, Jerry should also see if there is at least one other estimating technique he can use for validation. It sounds like he relied on expert opinions to prepare the original estimate. He could also estimate the work at a low level using his work breakdown structure (or his project schedule if he is at that level). Since the work is fairly repetitive on thousands of workstations, he could also look for some estimating algorithm that could lead to a logical and reasonable number.

Second, Jerry should look at his estimating assumptions. All estimates are based on a set of explicit and implied assumptions. This is a time to look for creative ways to get the work done with less cost and effort, such as the following:

- **Look for less-costly alternatives**: This means looking at all costs associated with the project to see if less-expensive alternatives exist that will accomplish the same thing. For instance, if you are counting on contract labor resources, you can see whether they could be replaced with employees. If you are proposing new software, see whether your company already has something that will work. You could evaluate whether existing hardware can be utilized rather than buying new machines. If you have training costs in your budget, see whether the training can be done in-house instead of sending people to formal off-site classes. Remember, the purpose of this step is to see if there are alternatives that will allow you to reduce costs while still delivering all the required functionality.

- **Look for process improvements**: This step involves looking at how you propose to do the work to see if alternative approaches or techniques exist that will result in less effort and cost. For instance, if you have trips planned, determine whether some or all of the work can be accomplished with phone calls or teleconferences. See whether some manual processes can be automated. Perhaps a focused group meeting can be utilized to gather requirements instead of traditional one-on-one interview sessions. It may be possible to outsource some of the work at less cost than it would take to do it internally. Again, the purpose of this step is to deliver as planned while requiring less effort.

- **Negotiate a reduction in scope**: The two preceding options allow you to deliver all the work requested for less effort and cost than was originally proposed. This third option looks for activities or parts of the project that can be eliminated. Removing work should result in reduced effort and cost. Although all of the work on the project may have originally been seen as important, it usually turns out some components of the project are more important than others. In some instances, work can be deferred until a later date, perhaps when a new budget is available. This may result in a less-than-perfect solution, but one still acceptable to your sponsor.

Jerry needs to go back and revisit the estimate with these points in mind. He may find there are ways to pare down the estimate while delivering much of what the company needs. This exercise is not meant to force him into committing to a project budget he does not believe in. It is simply meant as an honest effort to reduce the estimated cost and effort.

Jerry owes his manager a complete explanation of how the estimate was prepared. If, at the end of this process, Jerry's estimate is still too high, he must ask for the assistance of his manager and other stakeholders to determine whether or how to proceed.

One option is to not do the project at all. If the cost of doing the project is more than the perceived benefit, it simply should not be done. Management stakeholders may have other options, including requesting the required incremental budget dollars if they are convinced additional money is justified.

After seeing Jerry's second estimate, including reasonable alternatives and options, his manager can determine how to proceed. If Jerry's estimate is still too high, his manager will need to take the new number forward for approval or come up with some alternatives. If Jerry's estimate is closer to the original budget (even if the project scope has been reduced), his manager may be able to approve the work and let the project proceed. Either of these alternatives is better for Jerry and for the company than purposely underestimating the work—and then having to face the consequences later when the project goes over budget.

Don't Forget Face-to-Face Communication on Your Project

Jean Combs was a tall woman with long, blonde hair. Her husband, Rick, was the head football coach at Northeast Illinois State and a friend of my wife Pam. Their son Dan was the same age as Tim, and the two boys were friends. Jean was a quick learner when given new assignments, so when she called me to schedule an afternoon appointment, I knew something must have really stumped her on her project for the Finance department.

"Come in, Jean! Good to see you. How are Rick and Dan?"

"They are both well, thanks for asking. Rick is busy interviewing candidates for defensive line coach at the university now that Jordan McKenzie

has left for Purdue. He's a little worried since it is already July 1 and summer workouts are in progress. Of course, little Dan is still a bundle of energy and has recently taken an interest in golf."

"That's funny! Tim has also shown some interest in golf. We'll have to get the two of them together sometime and play miniature golf. We can form our own mini PGA Tour!"

"I am sure Dan would love that!"

"Tell you what, I'll give you a call over the weekend and we'll try to set something up. Now, what brings you to see me today?"

"Well, I could use some help on this project," she began. "It isn't in bad shape, but we missed a couple of milestone dates by less than a week. I think we are back on target now."

"That's good news," I said.

"Well, I wouldn't get too optimistic yet," she replied, trying to force a smile. "The overall schedule is very aggressive. What makes it frustrating is I received feedback from my sponsor and client manager recently saying we need to do a better job communicating what's going on. I've tried to communicate as much as possible, including sending out status reports. Not that anyone reads them."

"This project sounds very important to the Finance department," I said. "Why wouldn't they read the status reports?"

"It's just the way this project has gone," she replied, clearly frustrated. "I don't think anyone reads the status reports. When we sent out e-mails to solicit requirements, we received very few replies. I send out e-mails whenever we have problems, but I don't get any help from the senior managers. We also publish risk plans, project news, and current status on a shared web server, but very few clients read it. I think it's unfair of them to say now we are not communicating effectively."

I see a pattern here. "It certainly sounds like you have provided the clients with a lot of information," I noted. "However, when is the last time you met with them face to face?"

LESSON

One of the key responsibilities of a project manager is to communicate proactively to clients, team members, and stakeholders. Some of this communication is routine and obvious, including status meetings and status reports. However, status meetings and status reports are the minimum expectation for communicating on a project. These communication updates help to manage expectations, but they do not satisfy the total communication needs for most projects. If your project is large and impacts a substantial number of people, a Communication Plan should be created to meet the needs of all stakeholders.

Since proactive communication is probably not her strong suit, Jean has found herself communicating in a manner that best suits her needs and not the needs of her clients and stakeholders. The approach is based purely on an electronic medium. Sure, it's easier to fire off e-mail messages. Yes, it might be quicker to place documentation on a shared web server for stakeholders to read. But the truth is these forms of communication are only easier and quicker for Jean and they do not address the needs of her clients at all.

To be fair, there is nothing wrong with Jean's communication. There is a place for e-mail messages, status reports, and collaborative web sites. They are vital pieces in an overall Communication Plan. However, they should not be used as a way to avoid meeting with your sponsor and client managers. There is no substitute for face-to-face meetings and personal communication.

Jean is facing a common IT problem. She is providing information, but it is not always delivered effectively. She is comfortable working with her team members and the lower-level client users, but she is not as comfortable talking with the more senior client stakeholders.

Jean needs to understand that senior managers can receive hundreds of messages per day. They also have many initiatives going on simultaneously. Jean's project is important to them, but they have many other competing priorities. It is not reasonable to assume they will always be able to sift through hundreds of e-mails to find the key bits of information relevant to the project.

This is not meant to be an excuse for them. The senior management stakeholders should have an interest in the project and should invest the time to make sure it has everything it needs to be successful. However, the project manager needs to make it easy for them. It is much more likely they will

will remember the things they hear at meetings and from colleagues, even if the information is not entirely accurate.

It certainly looks like Jean is communicating. However, she has not found the right forum and format to provide her clients with the information they want to know. That is why, in spite of the communication Jean has done, the clients are still telling her she needs to communicate more. Actually, it appears they would like Jean to communicate more *effectively* with them.

My advice to Jean is to ask the sponsor and client manager how she can best communicate to them. For instance, Jean may need to set up periodic briefings for the sponsor and other senior stakeholders. She might also create status updates that are in more of a business memo format. The e-mails and status reports will then be much more effective as a means of filling in the blanks between personal meetings. This will provide more accurate and reliable information for them and make them more comfortable communicating directly with her if they have further questions.

Make Quality a Mindset and Ongoing Process

I had been trying to cut back on my coffee intake lately. Not that I was "Mr. Healthy" but every little bit helped, I figured. Who needs all that caffeine anyway? Part of the plan was to avoid drinking coffee at home in the morning and instead drink water or juice. So my first cup was usually in my office as I checked my e-mail. This morning I was returning from the break room with my first cup when I ran into Erika Thompson.

Erika was wearing a black skirt with a red blouse and flag-shaped earrings (it was July 3). Her husband, Martin, was in the Army and was stationed overseas on an eight-month tour of duty. The Fourth of July was very meaningful to her because her father was killed in combat during the Vietnam War. She visited Washington, D.C., last year with her husband, and I remembered her saying it was a moving experience, especially visiting the Vietnam Memorial.

"I see you are ready for Independence Day," I said as she waved her hand at me.

"You bet I am, although it will be tough with Martin away from home."

"When does his tour of duty end, Erika? Seems like he has been gone for quite some time."

"He left right after Christmas last year, so he'll be back in a few months. I can hardly wait!"

"I bet. Your frantic wave makes me think you have something on your mind besides fireworks, though."

"You're right," she said, taking a deep breath. "I have heard you talk about the need for building quality into our solutions. I have a team building a new employee self-service module onto our benefits system. I wanted to let you know that we have just built a Quality Plan. We wanted to do something because Human Resources has a lot of sensitive information, and we need to make sure the information is accurate and secure."

I was pleased. "Great," I said. "I think you will find that building quality into your process will save you effort and cost over the entire project. Tell me about your plan."

"We have done a number of things," she explained. "First, we have a Quality Day scheduled every two weeks. That's the time we check the results of everyone's work to date. Second, we have designated a person to check the entire self-service application when it is complete to find any errors we may have missed. Third, we have asked one of our clients to be responsible for the overall quality of the solution. With these kinds of checks in place, we should end up with a good product."

I thought for a minute. On the surface, all of this sounded good, but something wasn't quite right. "Erika," I asked, "what are your developers doing in between the Quality Days?"

"They are working hard to build this module," she explained. "In fact, they think they can get more work done since they know reviews will be *done every other week and that someone will double-check the application at the end of the project."*

This was starting to confirm my suspicions. *"Let's talk a little further about your plan. Building quality into your solution needs to be an integral part of your development process. It appears you have a series of quality events, but you want to make sure people are taking personal responsibility for quality as well."*

LESSON

A good definition of quality management is that you understand what quality means to your client and you put a proactive plan in place to achieve that level of quality. This requires a combination of quality planning, quality control (inspection), and quality assurance (prevention). Repeatedly finding errors and fixing them (quality control) can result in a high quality product, but it is a very inefficient process. The best approach is to build a quality product the first time. In general, your team can't build a quality product the first time without quality work processes (quality assurance).

Building a quality product also requires a quality mindset. The team needs to be personally concerned about quality, and they need to take responsibility for building a quality product. The team needs to be constantly looking for ways to do things right the first time and looking for ways to capture any defects as early as possible after they have been introduced.

It appears Erika's team has great intentions. In fact, her approach may be better than doing nothing at all, since it does at least heighten everyone's awareness of the need for quality. However, she appears to have made three mistakes that may negate her team's good intentions.

First, although it's okay to focus on quality on a scheduled basis, she needs to ensure that her team doesn't see quality as a series of events. Her team members must see quality as a daily aspect of their job. Let's look at her biweekly Quality Days. On the surface, there is nothing wrong with this idea. However, consider Erika's comment about the team getting more work done because they can catch errors on Quality Days. Erika needs to make sure that her team members are not producing lower-quality work because they see Quality Day as a net in which to catch errors. If this is the case (and it sounds like it is), her team members are not taking personal responsibility for getting their work done right the first time. They may also be viewing quality as a biweekly event instead of a continuous process. Furthermore, finding and fixing errors after the fact is inefficient. It is a direct cause of rework, which is a large time-waster on a project.

Second, they have designated a person to check all work at the end of the project. Again, this may be fine as long as it is a final inspection in an ongoing quality process. But, again, Erika needs to be sure team members are not producing work of poor quality based on the assumption that someone else is responsible for catching errors later on. Catching errors at the end of the project is better than not catching them at all, but generally this is the worst time to catch them. Errors caught at the end of the project are the most costly and time consuming to correct. Catching errors early is a much better approach. Her team should be conducting error checks as soon as deliverables are produced.

Third, designating a client to be in charge of overall quality appears to shift the responsibility. It's great that the client is involved. However, in a quality environment, the project team needs to be responsible for quality. In fact, each person must be responsible for his work. The client may be asked to help verify that the final product meets her expectations, but she should not be responsible for the work others are producing.

Erika's quality plan should be revised in these areas. First, she can schedule walkthroughs and testing inspections throughout the development process—not just at arbitrary biweekly Quality Days. Her team should understand that it is responsible for the work it produces—and that it can't assume others will catch their errors. Lastly, although clients can verify that the final solution meets their quality expectations, the overall responsibility for quality must remain with the team that is building the solution. These changes will ensure the team has a quality mindset and takes responsibility for the product it is building.

Batch Small Scope Change Requests for Sponsor Approval

Sean Robinson had been in the IT Application Support organization for almost 15 years and was one of the best. He knew our Marketing applications inside and out—and always knew where to find the answers if they weren't already in his head. Like many support specialists, however, Sean was not the strongest project manager. Perhaps that's the nature of good support people; they're used to jumping in and fixing problems quickly—a long activity for him might have been 20 hours. Maybe that was why it was tough for him to develop the patience and structured thinking required to plan and manage larger projects.

In spite of these shortcomings, Sean was often asked to manage projects to enhance current Marketing applications, and he had enough knowledge and experience to deliver small enhancement projects reasonably close to expectations. Sean was also open and willing to learn structured project management techniques—at least up to a point. I talked to Sean about his current project. He was a little apprehensive.

Sean said the purpose of his project was to track the response rates of direct mail campaigns. The project was projected to last four months and had started last month on June 15. Unfortunately, the project was already at risk of exceeding its budget and deadline. I asked a standard series of questions about how he was managing the project to see if I could identify some root causes for why the project was in trouble. I asked about the schedule, deliverables, risks, staffing, issues, etc. When we got to scope change management, Sean was a little defensive.

"You know, I am more than willing to use formal project management techniques when they make sense," Sean said, running his hand through his thick blonde hair. "But you know Marketing. They always want changes after agreeing to the initial scope. I would like to use good scope change management, but the changes are always small. You know, five hours here, three hours there. Pretty soon you are talking about some real hours. I think that's why we are in trouble."

"Let's talk about your scope change procedures," I said. "Can you tell me how you are managing these small changes?"

"Our scope management process normally includes gaining sponsor approval for changes," Sean said. "But am I the only person who has a busy sponsor? I can't take every two-hour scope change request to him. He would throw me out of his office. So we are trying to be client focused and fit as many of these small changes in as possible. What other options do I have?"

"Obviously, you don't want to bother your sponsor for every small scope change request," I said. "However, there's another option. Let's talk about this further."

LESSON

I can sympathize with Sean. He thinks he has done a good job establishing scope, and he is prepared to handle scope changes by taking the change requests to the sponsor, along with the project impact assessment. However, he also knows the sponsor is busy and thus hesitates to bother him with "minor" scope changes. Sean is probably right. Most likely, the sponsor does not want to be bothered with every two- and four-hour scope change request. There are a couple alternatives, however.

First, it may be perfectly acceptable for the project manager and the main client manager to have some discretionary power to approve small scope changes, as long as the changes do not impact the team's ability to deliver the project on time and within budget. Notice that a designated client representative must still agree to the scope change request. It is still not a project manager decision. The sponsor will need to agree to this delegation of authority and then it can be added to the scope change process. If small change requests are submitted, they must still be documented with estimates on project impact and business value. This process does not need to be elaborate. Each request could simply take up one line of the Scope Change Log.

Note the key caveat: this discretionary authority can be used only <u>if there is no impact on the project timeline and budget</u>. This doesn't help Sean, since he stated he is already at risk of going over schedule and budget.

In Sean's case, he should utilize a second project management technique for small changes—batching small scope changes together. This still means keeping track of the small scope changes, their business value, and their impact on the project. When they hit a certain threshold, he can take all of them to the sponsor for approval. The threshold could be reached when the impact of the scope changes exceeds a target, such as 100 hours. The threshold could also be in terms of the number of small requests received, such as 10 small requests.

The result is that instead of visiting the sponsor 10 times for 10 small scope changes, he batches them all together and sees the sponsor once for each batch of changes. At that meeting, Sean, the client manager, and the sponsor can discuss the proposed changes and get sponsor approval. The benefit of having the sponsor approve the changes is that he or she can also approve the incremental budget and time needed to get the work done.

Keep in mind, however, that just as this idea of batching requests may be new to the project manager, it may also be new to the sponsor. Therefore,

Sean needs to explain the process to the sponsor and get the sponsor's agreement on using this process to manage small scope change requests.

If you utilize this technique, you may find the sponsor has little patience and sympathy for small incremental scope change requests that add only small incremental business value. As mentioned in Chapter 11, sponsors typically do not want to be distracted from the main business objectives. If the final solution meets 80 percent of their needs, they are typically happy. They normally don't care to add too many small requests that may only result in the solution meeting 82 percent of their needs. These small changes are just a distraction. Although Sean might hesitate to say "no" to scope change requests, the sponsor typically does not have that problem. Usually they are more than happy to say "no."

Sean's last comment on being client focused is telling. His team is trying to be client focused by agreeing to include as many small changes as possible. However, is this really being client focused? If the project goes over budget and over its deadline, will the sponsor talk about Sean's amazing client focus? Probably not. Instead, the sponsor will talk about how the team missed its commitments.

The best thing Sean can do to be client focused is to meet his commitments on project budget and deadline. His major client is the sponsor. With his project now at risk, he should ensure no changes are agreed to without sponsor approval and without a corresponding increase in budget and schedule.

Manage Your Vendor Projects Proactively

Pam and I took Tim to the department store to shop for back-to-school items. Although was still July, Tim was starting kindergarten in the fall and we wanted to spark some excitement in him by buying a few supplies. The school sent us a welcome pack over the summer, including a sheet of required tools—the usual fare of pencils, pens, glue, crayons, scissors, etc. The first thing we bought was a black-and-red backpack with golf balls on it. Tim and I had been practicing golf quite a bit over the summer and I promised to take him to a real course next year.

Leaving the department store, we drove to the Morettis' old house to have dinner with Jerry and Barbara. I was excited to see what they had done with it. As we pulled into the driveway, I could already see one big change. Jerry had pulled the bushes out from around the house and replaced them with flower gardens. There was also a nice bed of flowers planted around the mailbox.

"Looks like Jerry and Barbara have added some flower power!" I said to Pam as we approached the front door.

On the inside, things were mostly the same, but with all new furniture. Jerry said they were still going to paint but decided to plant the flowerbeds first to take advantage of the nice weather. "Good project management decision," I said jokingly. Jerry led me down to the basement where I was surprised to see the shelves covered in beer steins, just as they were when Wayne lived there.

"I thought that might surprise you," Jerry said as I looked around. "A nice gift from Wayne. He left me all his beer steins. He said he didn't have much use for them in Arizona, and he knew how much I admired them when I saw them for the first time. I told Wayne I would continue to display them and that he should let me know if he ever decided he wanted them back."

"That was incredibly thoughtful of Wayne," I said, admiring a stein with a Harley Davidson motorcycle on the front. "Of course, it doesn't really surprise me. Wayne is a great guy."

Jerry showed me some of his favorite steins and then grabbed a couple beers out of the refrigerator in the bar. Handing one to me, he asked if I would mind talking shop for a few minutes. He was still in the early stages of his new project to deploy an operating system upgrade on all of our desktops, and he said his head was swimming with too much information.

"As you can imagine, the technical considerations for this project are not difficult," Jerry began carefully. "Upgrading a workstation is easy. However, when you have thousands of workstations, the complexity of completing the entire project starts to get overwhelming. We are outsourcing the majority of the project to one of our vendors. I initially thought the vendor would take care of everything; however, they still want me to make the overall decisions on schedule, priorities, risks, etc. My boss has also told me I am still responsible for the success of this project—even though a vendor is doing most of the work."

"I think that makes sense," I said. "In the past, people thought that if you outsourced a project, you outsourced the problems as well. This is definitely not the case. As the client company, we need to maintain overall responsibility and ownership of the project."

"You're right," Jerry agreed. "But how do I manage these vendor re-sources? They have their own project manager, their own schedule, and their own plan. It's hard enough to manage my own staff. How can I keep track of the work when it is managed by a vendor?"

"The interesting thing about managing outsourced work is that it is not too much different than managing your own internal staff. Let's talk about this a little more."

LESSON

Outsourcing of project work is more and more common. In the past, many companies experienced poor results from outsourcing. This partly reflected the inability of the vendor companies to successfully deliver against the contract. However, it was also partly due to the inability of the client company to manage the outsourced relationship proactively. Many companies felt that if they outsourced the work, they also outsourced the problems. They also felt like they outsourced responsibility and accountability to the vendor.

The better approach is to recognize that you have a project and you are still responsible for it. You may outsource some of the work to a vendor. In fact, you may outsource the majority of the work, or all of the work, to a vendor. However, you still have overall responsibility for the project. If all goes well with the vendor, you do not have much work to do. Unfortunately, in many instances, the vendor does not perform against expectations. You need to be proactively managing the project so that you know about any problems as soon as possible.

Many people are not sure what to do when asked to manage a vendor relationship. Part of the uncertainty stems from the project roles being reversed. On a normal internal project, the Project Manager assigns the work and manages issues, scope, risk, quality, etc. The Project Manager makes sure work is done on time and that the project is progressing. He is held accountable for the success of the project.

On an outsourced project, the vendor's Project Manager should be the one who is worried about the project management details. The vendor's Project Manager is planning and assigning the work as well as managing issues, scope, risk, etc.

In this situation, the client Project Manager takes on a quality assurance role to monitor the vendor work. This is the role Jerry should take on his project. Fortunately, he understands the basics of project management. He just needs to apply this knowledge toward monitoring the vendor. Let's look at the following examples:

- **Schedule:** Jerry knows he needs a schedule on his projects. He should therefore understand that the vendor Project Manager needs a schedule as well. Just as Jerry needs to keep the schedule current, he should validate that the vendor's Project Manager is keeping the schedule current.
- **Scope:** Jerry knows how to manage scope on his projects. He needs to ensure the vendor is doing the same.
- **Communication:** Jerry needs to make sure there is regular and effective communication between his team and the vendor team—just as he makes sure his team communicates effectively with his client.
- **Risk:** The vendor needs to be assessing and managing risks. After all, if the vendor identifies risks, they are also potential risks for Jerry.

You get the pattern now. Jerry is initially unsure how to manage the vendor, but in essence, he manages the vendor the same way he would manage his own projects. He needs to validate that the vendor's Project Manager is managing the work proactively. This includes staying on schedule, meeting milestone dates, communicating effectively, managing scope, building to acceptable levels of quality, etc. If Jerry can validate that this is happening on the vendor project, chances are the vendor project will complete successfully. On the other hand, if there are problems on the vendor project (and many times there are), Jerry will know about them early, which provides more options for solving them. In either case there is a greater likelihood that the project will have a successful outcome.

Look for Risks Inherent to Your Project

The last week of July was hot and muggy in Dickens. The weatherman predicted rain for the weekend but said that the week would bring high humidity and temperatures in the 90s. Pam was attending a sports conference in Chicago, and Tim and I had plans for a "guy's weekend" of eating pizza and watching the Cubs play a series at Cincinnati on TV. Tim liked watching the Cubs play, although he still had a hard time sitting through nine innings of baseball. By about the fourth inning, I usually had to pull out a deck of cards or a board game.

I had just ended a phone call with Pam when Danielle Bartlett came by for her 11 a.m. meeting. When I last saw her, she was dressed from head to toe in black for Valentine's Day. This time she wore a colorful skirt and blouse and appeared to be much happier. I asked her why she was so happy.

"Well, believe it or not, I met a guy on Valentine's Day, and we've been dating for the last five months," she said. "I met him buying beer at the grocery store. Turns out we were both alone on the dreaded day, so we got to talking and the rest is history."

"Wow, that's exciting," I replied. "And if things work out well, your boyfriend will never forget the details of how you guys met. After all, it was Valentine's Day and there was beer involved!" I chuckled.

"I guess you're right," she agreed. "Plus for me, the day is that much more romantic since it's the day we met."

"Well, I am glad to see you so happy. Also, I believe more congratulations are in order. I heard your project to implement a construction cost-estimating package was completed without a hitch."

"Thanks," Danielle smiled back. "However, I don't know if that was a good move or not. My boss thanked me by asking me to manage another project for the Facilities Department. Oh well, I guess that's why they pay me the big bucks!"

"Well, 'Ms. Big Bucks,' what have they got you doing now?"

"The Facilities department works with a number of vendors and subcontractors. They think they can coordinate their work more effectively if they have a small intranet portal available that all the vendors can link into. Then everyone can get common information and coordinate schedules more effectively."

"Great news!" I said in a purposely half-sarcastic tone.

"Hardly," she said, taking a seat in the chair in front of my desk. "I've been talking with the business clients and with my team members," she began. "They keep telling me this is a low-risk project and I should not be worried. But I am very uncomfortable right now."

"Why are they saying this is a low-risk project?" I asked.

"The people from Facilities know their business very well," she replied, fanning herself with a file folder. "They think they can create the content for this web site portal with a minimum of effort from our IT team. We just need to set up the secure environment to begin with. In the short term, however, many of the clients are starting to work on a major office renovation. They are using spreadsheets and e-mail to coordinate *work with the vendors and say anything would be better. The IT project team just wants to get going. They think they can overcome any problems that might pop up."*

"That's the kind of approach that can get you into trouble," I said. "Sure, problems can be fixed, but at what cost to budget, schedule, and quality? What other things are making you uncomfortable?"

"I only have a few months' experience with new web technology and the two people on my team have less than me," Danielle answered. "This is also my first opportunity to manage a substantial web project that requires third-party access. When I did background checking, I read about other companies having problems with this particular release. And besides that ..."

"Whoa!" I interrupted. "Hold on a minute. I heard three or four risks in the last minute alone. I think you are right to be concerned about the overall project risk. It seems you are just having a hard time isolating the risks and articulating them. Let me find a risk assessment form for you to look at. It contains characteristics of projects that bring inherent risks with them. Once you have identified all your high risks, you can put risk plans in place to respond to them."

LESSON

Sometimes it's easy to look at a project and see risks. For instance, you may have a fixed deadline that will be hard to achieve. This is a risk that is easy to see because it's generic. It's not specific to your project. In fact, any project with a tight deadline will have some risk associated with the schedule. These types of generic risks are called *inherent risks*.

When you are identifying risks on your project, the first place to look is the inherent risks. Some project characteristics, by their very nature, imply higher risk. Another example of inherent risk is project size. A project requiring 500 effort hours has less inherent risk than one requiring 5,000 effort hours, or one requiring 50,000 hours. If you knew nothing else at all about the project, you could say the larger project of 50,000 hours is riskier than the project of 500 hours. More effort hours means more people to manage, more budget to control, and more chances for staff turnover. In general, there is more of a chance for people-related problems. Increased complexity in any form typically means increased inherent risk.

Other inherent risks include using new vendors, implementing new technology, having vague requirements, and using an inexperienced project team. These are examples of risks that are not specific to a single project. They would increase the risks on any project.

Let's look at Danielle's project. She is uneasy about the risks associated with it. Her client is telling her it's no big deal, but she knows better. Based on the discussion, her project has the following potential risks:

- She and her team are inexperienced with new web technology, which makes for more risk than if they had experienced people on the team. This is an example of an inherent risk, since any project is riskier if the team is inexperienced.
- This is Danielle's first opportunity to manage a substantial project that requires interaction with vendors. Her lack of experience could be a big risk. This is also an example of an inherent risk, since any major project with an inexperienced project manager will be riskier than one with an experienced project manager.
- It appears the client may not have the time to focus on this project because of another large initiative. There is an inherent risk whenever there is a question about the commitment of your client.

Inherent risks are based on the general characteristics of a project rather than the specific circumstances of your project. Since they are general in nature, they can be identified and placed in a checklist for all project managers to review. This should be the starting point for the risk identification process. If you identify an inherent risk, determine whether it is a high risk for your project or something lower. If you find high risks (or perhaps medium risks), it does not mean that the project should not go forward. It simply means the project manager should focus risk plans in those areas of identified risk to minimize the potential for problems during the project.

Get Sponsor Approval Before Investigating Large Scope Change Requests

Mike Miller and I had not worked together for several months but we got together for some basketball last weekend at a park near my house. After the game, he mentioned some problems with a new project to install document management software at our worldwide regional headquarters. In fact, his team had fallen behind on the project. A very laidback guy, Mike didn't appear to be too worried about the delays, but I asked him to drop by my office on Tuesday to discuss things.

"Come on in Mike. Thanks for the game last weekend!"

"Sure thing, Coach. Hope you weren't too sore that night!" Mike was a bit of a bruiser, especially on the boards. Every time he missed a shot, he banged into me as I tried to get the rebound. It was a friendly game but with a lot of physical contact. I was a bit sore after our game, but I wasn't about to admit it.

"I felt great. There's nothing like a little basketball in August to get you sweating. I haven't played that hard since my college days!" I replied.

"Wow, has it really been 30 years?" Mike said before bursting into laughter.

"Wow, I really tossed you a softball there. Nice job smacking it out of the park!"

'Thanks, Coach. Just pulling your leg as always."

"I know. After the game you mentioned you were falling behind on your project. What's the story there?"

"Actually, we aren't too bad right now, but we have just received a change request that may cause us some trouble. You know we recently installed document management software for the Legal department here in the headquarters. Now we have a new project to install a similar system for our other Legal departments in Tokyo and London. However, our London client has some off-the-wall ideas that will require making substantial customizations to the standard package because of some differences in how the London office operates."

"A substantial change could require replanning the entire project," I replied. *"I hope you invoked your scope change procedures. This is clearly something not envisioned when your project started."*

"Yes, it's definitely a scope change," Mike agreed. *"Unfortunately, I can already see where this is heading. We can't make a change of this magnitude and still hit our end-of-year deadlines for completing both offices. So, we will spend two weeks looking at the impact to the project and preparing a cost estimate. I'm certain the change request will not be approved, but we will still be held accountable for hitting our original delivery date."*

"Do your scope change procedures say anything about how much time you will spend on investigations?" I asked.

"No," Mike said. "They only say we will investigate the request to de-termine the impact to the project in terms of effort, cost, and duration. The sponsor will then decide if we proceed or not."

"That sounds like a good beginning, but you've missed something," I concluded. "There is another scope change request that needs to be taken to your sponsor."

Mike looked puzzled. "What other scope change?" he asked.

"This may be hard to follow at first," I said. "But the analysis required for the scope change is itself a scope change. It is a substantial piece of work you did not count on, and it will impact your effort and sched-ule. You need to check with the sponsor before even undertaking the investigation."

"Wow, that's a great insight and you are obviously right on. Thank God your project management is better than your basketball!"

Walked into another one.

LESSON

When you create your initial project estimates, you need to include time and effort hours for project management activities. On most projects, the rule of thumb is that project management will take 15 percent of the project effort hours. For instance, if you estimate a project to take 1,000 effort hours, the time allocated for project management would be around 150 hours, making the final estimate 1,150 effort hours. This covers the time it takes to manage the schedule, assign work, communicate effectively, manage risks, etc. The time it takes to manage the scope change process is included in this percentage as well.

The 15 percent rule assumes you have typical project management activities. It is possible to go over that amount, depending on the type of manager you are. Also, some project management activities can increase that percentage. For instance, if your project plan is complex or if you have to replan the work based on resource changes, you could easily reach 20 or 25 percent.

Scope change requests would not normally require you to exceed your pro-ject management estimates. Typically, you just need to guide the requests through the scope change process. If the scope changes are approved, you should receive the appropriate budget and schedule adjustments.

Some scope change requests, however, require a substantial amount of time to investigate and to estimate. These relatively large scope change requests are not taken into account in the 15 percent project management guideline. For instance, let's look again at the earlier example of a project that requires 1,000 effort hours and 150 hours for project management. If you receive a major scope change request that will take 80 hours to investigate, you are obviously going to have trouble fitting it within your project management time.

The project manager needs to recognize the potential impact on a project when a request comes in requiring scope change management. The project manager must also recognize the impact that the investigation associated with a scope change request may have on the project. If the scope change investigation is significant, the project manager must engage the sponsor very early in the scope change process. The sponsor needs to understand the nature of the request and then decide if the value of the investigation is worth the impact to the project. If the sponsor agrees to the impact, they should provide the necessary schedule and budget relief, since this magnitude of investigation is not covered in the normal project management allocation.

Mike is in that position today. His project management budget was not built to take into account a major scope change investigation like this. Since this is unanticipated work, the investigation itself is out of scope. Rather than charge ahead with the investigation, Mike should take this request to the sponsor immediately. In essence, he should follow his normal scope change management process. Unless the business value is high enough to approve the impact on schedule and budget, the sponsor will probably reject the request and leave the original scope intact. If Mike is correct in his view that his sponsor would probably not approve the software customizations, it is likely he will not approve the scope change investigation either. However, if the sponsor does approve the investigation and its impact on the project, the budget and schedule can be adjusted to account for this additional work.

Make Sure the Cost of Collecting Metrics Does Not Exceed Their Value

Charles Riley was an intense man with a great sense of humor who was known to work very long hours. His colleagues had nicknamed him "Chucky" after the crazy doll portrayed in the movie Child's Play because of his intensity and laser beam focus. I had never met him but had been told by a colleague that his reputation for being intense was justified. My colleague also said he was a very funny man who appreciated a good joke and loved telling one. I was looking forward to our meeting.

He arrived right on time for our 2 p.m. meeting.

"Come on in, Charles," I said as I stood to shake his hand. "How are you today?"

"I'm doing okay, Tom; thanks," he said, sitting quickly. "I have to tell you, though, that I'm having a bit of trouble with this current project of mine. We're doing some work with the Payroll department and I could use your help."

I noticed as he spoke that he held his hands firm and rigid and frequently darted them out and then up and down, like he was trying to karate chop an imaginary board in front of him. As expected, he was definitely intense, although I was beginning to think his "Chucky" nickname more accurately referred to Chuck Norris.

"Tell me more about this project and let's see if I can offer any counsel," I said.

He explained that his team was nearing the midpoint on a project to develop a new employee datamart for Payroll. Part of the business justification for this project was the productivity increase that would result from the payroll managers being able to write their own ad-hoc requests for information. The sponsor wanted Charles to try to measure this benefit. This required estimating the time it took to gather information today using the manual spreadsheets. This baseline information would be used to see whether the new datamart software was more efficient.

"We built time into our schedule to collect these productivity metrics, but we only allocated time for members of the project team. We didn't take into account the time needed by the payroll managers. These managers are complaining about having to measure and track this information. They are busy and don't have the time to spare to collect a lot of extra information."

"What information are you trying to collect?" I asked.

"We gave them a template to track how long it currently takes to find the information that they need, so that we can compare it with the *length of time it takes with the new software. The problem is the users get many requests each week, and it takes extra diligence to stop and document what they are doing."*

"Well, maybe they have a point. Everything we do on a project, including the collection of metrics, needs to make sense from a cost/benefit perspective," I said. "How much time does it take to fill out the template?"

"Some of the people are saying it takes a lot of time. But we're not really sure right now," he replied.

"You need to start by understanding the time and cost of collecting the metrics. Sometimes people don't like to do new things based on emotion and a resistance to change. However, sometimes the pushback is based on facts. It may, in fact, be disruptive to their daily routine. Your team will need to dig deeper to understand the effort associated with the collection of this metric and then work with your sponsor to make sure the value received is worth this effort. I'm not suggesting it is too much time. I am only saying you should estimate the impact of collecting the metrics before you start."

LESSON

Collecting meaningful data to help make business decisions is a good thing. In fact, most organizations would be better off if they had more information about how they are doing their jobs. However, the value attained by collecting this information has to be analyzed in light of the costs of collecting this information. It's a problem if the time and cost to collect the data is greater than the value of the resulting information.

The best metrics are those easily generated by a computer. They are automatically collected at a certain time, and reports can be generated from this data to show information in many ways. For instance, your company may tie costs against a project through your General Ledger System. If this is the case with your company, you'll find it relatively easy to gather information on how you are doing against your budget.

Project teams, however, don't usually have the time to create automated systems to collect customized metrics. Even if you have the time, the cost to develop these custom applications is not normally worth the resulting value of the metrics you collect. Therefore, most of the metrics reported on a project are collected manually.

There are three questions to ask regarding those metrics requiring manual collection efforts.

1. How much effort and cost does it take to gather the information?

2. Are there less expensive, alternative metrics that will approximate the same result?

3. Is the value of the knowledge gained worth the effort and cost?

As usual, the definition of value is a matter of opinion—usually the sponsor's.

Charles needs to ask these questions today. His sponsor would like to get some hard numbers on the productivity gains associated with the new application. Charles and his team have come up with a way to determine this value by comparing the time it takes using the manual processes today with the time that it will take to complete the same function with the new solution in place.

Charles has a good solution, but it may come at too high a price. He and his team need to do some analysis into the time and cost associated with having the users complete the reporting templates. If the time is very short, he can proceed to the third question and ask the sponsor if the cost of collection is worth the benefit.

On the other hand, Charles is already getting feedback that the time taken to collect the information is high. This does not answer the third question since the sponsor is the one who makes the final decision—not the payroll managers. The payroll managers may not think the value is there, but the sponsor may have other ideas. However, it would be to Charles's benefit to look for some alternatives. For instance, if the payroll managers collect the information for two days per week, can the total time estimate be extrapolated from there? Perhaps Charles can ask each person to estimate the amount of time he or she spends performing the activity at the end of each day. This would be less accurate, but the effort—and therefore the cost of collection—would be reduced considerably as well.

Once Charles has more information on the cost of collecting the metrics, as well as some alternatives, he should ask the sponsor for feedback on how to proceed. It may be that the sponsor is willing to have people collect very accurate data because of the resulting business value. Alternatively, the sponsor may decide having less accurate data, but at substantially reduced collection costs, is the way to go. In either case, Charles will find it easier to collect the metrics since the sponsor made the decision on how to capture the data.

Use Multiple Estimating Techniques

Alex Jordan was a divorced 45-year old father of two teenage boys. I had limited interaction with him on the job, but when we did talk I found him to be shy and nervous. He seemed to be more comfortable behind a computer screen than in front of people. Still, he seemed like a nice guy and no one had ever said anything bad about the quality of his work. He knocked on my door around 1:30 p.m. for our meeting to discuss his project.

Alex was responsible for a project to upgrade an old version of our standard database management software. First, he needed to put together an estimate of the effort required to complete the project.

"I need to put together a high-level estimate for this project, and I am having a hard time figuring out where to begin. We have more than 200 databases in our environment, and they each bring their own complexities. I don't have time to do 200 individual estimates."

I asked about estimating by analogy. "Have you discussed the project with the people who were responsible for installing the previous release? If you knew how much effort they had used, you might be able to estimate the effort for this one."

"I wish that were the case," Alex sighed. "However, the vendor is already telling us this new release will require a substantially larger amount of effort compared to that required for the previous release. I will be talking with the people who did the last upgrade, but it doesn't appear that their experience can be leveraged for this project."

Next, I thought about estimating based on expert opinion. "Okay, is it possible to find someone else who has gone through this before? Perhaps a database vendor or one of the research analysts could provide some insight."

"I'm afraid not," Alex sighed again. "We are one of the first companies to install the new release. The vendor is willing to help, since we will be one of their beta sites, but they don't want to put an estimate on the table because they don't know what our learning curve will be."

"Okay then, let's try a modeling approach since much of the work will be similar once we understand exactly what is required," I explained. "We can do a paper migration for a complex, medium, and simple database and then apply some fairly easy math to estimate the total project effort."

LESSON

Many people have an intuitive sense for the effort associated with certain types of work. Usually it's because they have done similar work in the past. However, when the work gets outside their comfort zone, they don't know how to put a logical estimate together.

Fortunately there are a number of formal techniques to estimate work. It is hard to say whether one approach is always better than another. It depends on the project and the information available. There are some very complex and mathematically driven estimating techniques, but there are a number of simpler ones as well. The following techniques can be used at a project level or activity level:

- **Previous history**: This is the best way to estimate work. If your organization keeps track of actual effort hours from previous projects, you may have information to help you estimate new work. Unfortunately, Mega Manufacturing, like most companies, does not save actual effort hours for prior projects. So, Alex will not be able to use this specific technique.

- **Analogy**: Even if you don't keep actual effort hours from previous projects, you may still be able to leverage previous work. Analogy means you look for similar projects, even if you don't capture and save all of the relevant details. This may just mean sending an e-mail to various department managers describing your project and asking if they know of any similar projects. If you find one, you can see if the project manager can estimate the effort hours on the project, and you can use the information as input for your estimate. Alex initially tried this approach by talking to people who worked on the last database upgrade, but it appears their experience will not be applicable on this project.

- **Ratio**: Ratio is similar to analogy except you have some basis for comparing work with similar characteristics, but on a larger or smaller scale. For instance, you may find the effort required to complete a software installation at the Miami office was 500 hours. If there are twice as many people in the Chicago office, you may be able to deduce that the Chicago installation will take 1,000 hours. Actually, Alex can take advantage of this technique. He can gather information on the effort hours it took the prior team to complete the upgrade and use that as a floor for his estimate. He would not expect his estimate to come at a lower level than this prior, less complex, upgrade. He knows his project is larger, so his effort hours should be larger as well.

- **Expert opinion**: In many cases, you may need to go to an internal or external expert to get help estimating the work. Although this may be your first time estimating a certain piece of work, perhaps someone else has done it many times. Alex has tried this technique as well. He asked the vendor for help estimating the time to upgrade databases because he was hoping they might have experts. The vendor declined to provide an estimate, since they did not have much experience with this release of their software. In fact, they would like Mega Manufacturing to be a beta site so they can gain experience from our project.

- **Work breakdown structure (WBS)**: The WBS approach involves breaking work down into smaller pieces. You may look at a large piece of work and have difficulty estimating the effort required. However, if the work is broken into smaller pieces, the individual components will be easier to estimate. When you have estimated all the smaller pieces, add them together for the overall estimate of effort. If you have the time to create a good WBS, you will usually end up with a good estimate. In this case, the WBS approach is probably not the best one for Alex. His WBS is probably not going to be very complicated. The estimating complexity is based on having to repeat the conversions so many times.
- **Parametric modeling**: In this technique, you look for a pattern in the work so an algorithm or model can be used to drive the overall estimate. For instance, if you know you can build one mile of flat, one-lane highway for $1 million, you should be able to easily calculate an estimate for ten miles of flat, four-lane highway ($40 million).

I think Alex can use a parametric modeling approach for this estimate. He has 200 instances of database upgrades to perform. Although each of these instances is unique, there will obviously be many similarities as well. Alex needs to identify a number of unique cases he can use to categorize all 200 database conversions.

My recommendation to Alex is to identify a very simple and small database, a very complex and large database, and one in the middle. For each of these databases, Alex can do a detailed work breakdown analysis to estimate what it will take to migrate to the new release. Next, he will look at the entire population of databases and categorize them into similar groups of complex, medium, and simple. This may require some help from the other members of the DBA staff (it doesn't matter whether a few are misplaced, since it will not materially affect the overall estimate). Then, he just needs to multiply the number of complex databases by the estimate required to convert one, and do the same with the medium and small categories. Finally, he will total up the time for database conversion, add the time required for project management, and add an additional percentage for estimating contingency. The numbers might look like the following table:

Table 34-1. Alex's Estimating Table

	Effort to Convert One Database	Approximate Number of Databases This Size	Total Effort
Small	8	55	440
Medium	15	112	1,680
Large	20	34	680
Total Conversion Effort		201	2,800
Project Management	15%		420
Subtotal			3,220
Estimating Contingency	10%		322
Total			3,542

When Alex is done, he will have a fairly scientific, defendable estimate for upgrading all 200-plus databases. He used a combination of at least three techniques:

- Expert opinion to estimate the effort for small, medium, and large databases.
- Ratio to ensure that the larger the database, the more effort it would take.
- Modeling to create and apply a model to estimate 201 conversions based on three estimates.

The logic for the estimate seems sound and should be defendable if he is challenged.

Keep Your Schedule Up to Date

Tim started kindergarten the last week of August, and it was a very emotional time for all of us. Pam and I were worried he would have a hard time adjusting to school and we were positive he would cry when we dropped him off on his first day. It turned out that Pam and I cried more than he did! It's tough watching your child grow up, but it had not really hit us how much older he was getting until we watched him run away happily into the schoolhouse that first day.

I told my story to Sean Robinson on Friday when I bumped into him in the parking garage at the end of the day. We were both sneaking out a bit early to get a jump on the weekend. He was on his way to the gym for his nightly workout so he was changing into a pair of tennis shoes behind his car. I knew Sean was a bit of a health nut; he enjoyed things like wheat germ and carrot juice.

"You sound like a really good father, Tom," Sean said after I finished my story. "I'm curious, though; do you find any correlation between raising a child and managing a project?"

"If I could find the correlation I'd make a million bucks on the book!" I said with a laugh.

When the laughter died down, I asked Sean about his project.

"I remember your project duration was about four months," I said. "You've been working for two-and-a-half months, right? Seems like you should be seeing the end."

"You've got that right," Sean said confidently. "We are about 60 percent complete."

When a project manager gives me a percentage complete figure for any project, it always sets off a little alarm in my head. Percentages are usually a sign of some guesswork. It's not a bad thing to give a high-level estimate of the percentage complete, but I decided to explore this answer a little more.

"Sixty percent complete?" I asked. "Is this a number your project management software generates?"

"No. But it's my estimate of where we are."

"Sean, when you and I met before, you had a good schedule that laid out the work to be completed. What's the schedule look like now?"

"Unfortunately it's not in as good a shape as it needs to be. We have been so busy lately I haven't even had time to update it."

"Well then, let me make a prediction," I said. "I predict your project will miss its deadline because I don't think you know exactly how much work is remaining."

LESSON

Everyone has heard the old adage "Plan the work, and then work the plan." It's a clever phrase and it's actually quite true. There is huge payback to the project if you first spend quality time defining the work and building a schedule. Defining the work ensures that you know what you are doing.

Building the schedule allows you to understand how the work will be accomplished.

The second part is important as well. You must work the plan. This means you must actually follow your plans, including the schedule, since it is your guide to completing the project.

This is the part that many project managers forget. The "plan the work, work the plan" cycle must be repeated throughout the project. It makes sense because you never know all of the details when you start a project. You can't foresee or control every possible event when the work is in progress. The overall plan, especially the schedule, will need to be modified over time.

There are two reasons to update your schedule. First, you need to validate the completed work and compare it to the work that was scheduled for completion. This gives you a sense of whether you are ahead, behind, or on schedule. Knowing where you are against your schedule allows you to put corrective plans in place if necessary. If you end up trending over your deadline date, you have much more flexibility if you catch the trend as early as possible.

The second reason for updating the schedule is to review the remaining work and to verify that you still understand the work required to complete the project. The nature of the project can change over time, especially if it is a large one. Changes are added, issues are resolved, new risks are identified, etc. The project manager must review the remaining work on a regular basis and ensure it is still an accurate reflection of the expected path to the completion of the project. If it's not, the schedule can be modified to reflect a better path to completion.

The duration of Sean's work is four months, and his schedule may not need the rigor of a multimillion-dollar project. However, he should still update his schedule every week. In fact, his schedule should have a weekly, one-hour activity assigned for him to update the schedule. If his schedule is not kept up to date, he really doesn't know if he will hit his end date and he doesn't know the work that remains to complete the project. It will be pure luck if his original schedule still reflects a valid path to completion.

When you ask project managers how a project is progressing, it's very common for them to give you a percentage complete. They are just trying to provide a sense of the amount of work completed and the amount remaining. There is nothing wrong with that.

However, project managers must understand where their project is on the overall schedule, as well as the activities remaining to complete the work. If a project starts to experience problems or starts to go over its budget and deadline, there may be a number of people who will suddenly become interested in going over the schedule in some level of detail.

Of course, in this case, I am one of the people interested in seeing an up-to-date schedule. When Sean said he was 60 percent complete, it was worth the follow-up questions from me to verify whether the estimate was based on fact or based on guesswork.

In general, not updating the schedule is simply the result of a lack of discipline. Sean probably thinks he is too busy on project-related activities to keep up on the project management activities. This is shortsighted and will probably end up putting his team in a time crunch when they realize, towards the end of the project, just how much work remains to be completed. Sean absolutely must update his schedule and keep it up to date. He may or may not end up meeting his project deadline, but the best way to know ahead of time is to update the schedule and ensure the remaining activities and estimates are accurate.

Use Issue Management to Choose the Best of Bad Alternatives

Lindsay Peterson stopped by my office in the first week of September to talk about her project to consolidate worldwide product sales for the Sales Department. I was trying to remember the last time I had spoken to her in an official capacity. After several minutes of thinking, I remembered it was the beginning of the year, shortly after the birth of her daughter Patricia. The Petersons lived just a few miles from Pam and I, and we often bumped into them at the local park or at the supermarket.

Lindsay was a good project manager and didn't often ask for counsel. I knew something big must have happened for her to visit with me.

"Come on in Lindsay! How is Patricia doing these days?"

"She's doing great. Still just as tiny and cute as can be. I still can't believe how different things are with her around."

"Well, just remember not to take any of this time for granted. You know, Pam and I took Tim to kindergarten last week. They grow up so fast."

"Believe me, I know. We're trying to take every day as it comes and enjoy the time as much as possible. We're definitely giving the camera a workout!"

"That's funny," I said as Lindsay sat down in the chair in front of my desk. "So let's talk about your project. Have you encountered a hurdle?"

"That's why I came to see you. We've run into a major problem," she began honestly. "A new software component that is part of our system doesn't work with the version of the web browser our company uses. The vendor component requires the new, updated browser version. We were initially told by our intranet support group that our company was going to migrate to this newer browser, but now the upgrade has been put on hold for at least three months."

"Hmmm. What have you done so far?"

Lindsay gave me a little history. "First of all, our testers raised this as a problem as soon as they realized the implications, and I notified our sales client right away. After initially being upset, they became engaged in the problem resolution process and we started looking for alternatives. First, we tried to get a version of the component that would run with the current browser, but the vendor doesn't have one. This is a new product for them, and they are not supporting older browser versions. Then we asked about upgrading the browser for our clients earlier than scheduled, but we were told we couldn't, since many other applications have not been tested with the new browser release yet. Then we talked to the client about removing the functionality the component provided, but they said the currency conversion calculations wouldn't work without it. We've looked at everything we can think of, but we must be overlooking something. What else should we be doing?"

"Have you met with your team and your client to brainstorm other alternatives and impacts?" I asked.

Lindsay was already ahead of me. "That's what we did first. Based on that meeting, we identified the alternatives that I have already mentioned. There are others we have looked at as well."

I thought for a second. "Lindsay, let me give you some bad news. The issues management process will help facilitate problem resolution if there is a good alternative to apply. However, it sounds like your remaining options are bad ones. At this point, you need to work with your client to make the best of a bad situation."

"In that case, let me ask you a favor," Lindsay said with a straight face. "Can I borrow your magic wand for a minute? I just want to make this project disappear."

LESSON

Issues are major problems that impede the progress of a project. They are different from normal problems because they can't be resolved without outside help. Usually, when problems arise on a project, there are some alternatives that will resolve the problem or help you to implement a workaround. In many cases, a number of viable solutions are available—you just need to find the best one. Sometimes the resolution will end up costing money and time. Sometimes a solution doesn't cost anything but the time you spend resolving it.

Applying good issues management techniques will help you to identify and resolve the problem. There are a number of good problem solving techniques that will help you to identify the cause, alternatives, and the best solution. Different techniques are used depending on the nature of the problem. Some examples of problem solving techniques include:

- *Pareto diagrams*, which help identify the 80/20 rule. These help you focus on identifying the 20 percent of the causes that are causing 80 percent of the problems. This is a good technique if there are multiple problems with many occurrences and you are trying to determine the relative impact of solving each problem.
- *"What-if" analysis*, which helps you determine the impact of solving certain aspects of the problem. This is a good technique for complex problems that need to be resolved through a variety of solutions.

- *Root cause analysis*, which guides you through a series of "why" questions until you find the actual cause of the problem. This is a good technique if the problem is relatively straightforward and if you feel there is ultimately one root cause.

Although proactively managing issues gives you the best chance to resolve them in a timely manner, the process doesn't guarantee that you will always find a satisfactory solution. Sometimes there is just no good alternative.

Let's review Lindsay's situation. First, a team member raised a problem as soon as it was discovered. Lindsay realized this problem was outside her team's ability to resolve, so she raised it as a formal project issue. She was able to get her client engaged in the problem resolution process. The entire team met to look at alternatives and came up with a prioritized list of potential solutions.

So far, Lindsay has done everything correctly. She has followed a good issues management process. However, the process has not resulted in an acceptable resolution. Some of the potential solutions are not possible, and some of the solutions are not acceptable to one or more of the major stakeholders.

Looking back, Lindsay might have helped herself out by identifying this as a potential risk earlier in the project. If it was identified as a risk, Lindsay could have monitored it much earlier and she may have taken a different approach to managing the risk. However, Lindsay did receive initial assurances that the Sales Division would be migrating to the newer browser on an earlier date, so she didn't feel it was a major risk at the time.

At this point, Lindsay needs to take one more look at whether there are any other ideas to resolve this successfully. If not, she and the client have no alternative but to identify the best solution causing the fewest problems. Perhaps the worst case scenario will be to stop (or to pause) the entire project until the situation is resolved. There might also be options to perform some work manually, or to delay some features until the browser is upgraded. They might also try escalating the problem to senior management to see if they can get the priority raised on the browser upgrade.

In any case, the client is not going to be happy with the outcome. At this point, the best alternative may be the one that inflicts the least pain and damage. It would be nice if every problem could be resolved with a satisfactory solution for everyone but sometimes it just doesn't work out that way. Since this is an issue, by definition it is impacting the project's ability to proceed. So, it has to be resolved—even if there are no perfect solutions.

CHAPTER

37

Collect Metrics That Can Lead to Fundamental Improvements

Terri Milner and Sarah York stopped by my office to discuss their new project. Terri and Sarah were sorority sisters in college and had recently been reunited because Sarah relocated to Dickens and began working at Mega Manufacturing in July. Terri had been with the company five years in June; she was generally respected for her intelligence but somewhat criticized for her lack of organizational skills. They were both very outgoing, and I was sure they were enjoying the opportunity to work together, even if the project assignment was out of the ordinary.

"So you guys were in the same sorority?" I asked when they came into my office.

"That's right," Terri offered. "Sarah and I were both Tri-Delts and really good friends. We hung out together a lot in college and took the same classes. It's been great to reconnect after so many years!"

"It's funny because Terri and I reconnected right away. It's like we didn't even skip a beat," Sarah said, grasping Terri's right hand. "We're like sorority sisters all over again."

"Maybe you guys can start a new Greek system here at Mega Manufacturing" I said jokingly. The two look at each other very seriously and nod in approval. "That would be amazing!" Terri said. After a few seconds of silence, they both shouted in unison. "Not!"

"Well, why don't you guys bring me up to speed on your project," I offered, moving the conversation back to work.

Terri and Sarah had been asked to put metrics in place to measure the overall satisfaction of Manufacturing Department users who call the IT help desk. Terri gave me some background about the effort while Sarah twirled her pen in her hand.

"Tom, you know we just installed our manufacturing software at the new plant," Terri began. "We expect there will be problems whenever a new package goes in. However, it's September and there still seems to be an unusually large number of problems on this installation. The IT team has resources dedicated to getting the bugs ironed out, but we could be dealing with a high number of support calls for many months. The problems are currently all over the board, and they are not sure what to expect next."

"I see," I replied. "It sounds as if your client wants to get more information on the impact that these problems are having on their staff."

"You're right. The plant manager is not happy with the problem resolution process," Sarah jumped in. "Since the plant is located outside the corporate environment, they have difficulties getting calls logged in the help desk. They think they are waiting too long for return calls and they are also not happy with the resolution of many of the problems. They think the same problems are occurring over and over again."

"What does the help desk say?" I asked, not sure whom to direct the question to.

"Actually, this gets at one of the primary reasons for setting up the metrics process," Terri explained. *"The help desk and the IT support group think they are responding in a timely manner. They say they have beefed up the staffing to help respond to the needs of the plant. However, no one knows for sure because we don't have any quantifiable numbers."*

When people can't agree on what is perception and what is reality, it's difficult to find the causes of problems. However, in this case, it appeared that everyone was simply looking to verify the facts so that proper decisions could be made. The help desk, IT support team, and the plant manager were all supportive of this effort.

"You were asked to define a set of metrics and how best to capture them." I recapped to Terri and Sarah. *"What are you proposing so far?"* Terri gave me the initial list. *"We want to collect information on the time that it takes to reach a live person on the help desk, on the time that it takes until an initial follow-up call from the support group is received, and on the time that it takes to resolve the problem. We also want to collect client survey metrics on the professionalism, knowledge, and courtesy of the help desk and support people."*

"That sounds like a great start," I agreed. *"But you're missing an additional set of metrics that are even more important."*

LESSON

Three major groups are collaborating on this project—the help desk, IT support team, and the manufacturing plant manager. All of them are interested in getting more facts about the problems coming out of the new plant and on the process that will help to resolve them in a timely manner. They are all frustrated because they don't have a common set of perceptions. The IT support team and the help desk say they have increased their capabilities to help the plant when problems arise. The plant management and staff think they are not getting a timely enough response. So, they are all partnering now to come up with some facts to help make decisions.

On the surface, the metrics Terri and Sarah are proposing look fine. In fact, there is nothing wrong with them. The metrics they have identified so far provide a sense of the service level of the help desk and the IT support staff. The plant manager wants to be sure his people's problems are being resolved in a timely manner, and the proposed metrics will certainly give him better information in that area.

The question is whether these metrics get at the root causes of the problems the client is experiencing. Terri and Sarah are not proposing any metrics to provide insight into the cause or causes of the problems. They are only proposing to measure how fast the problems are resolved once they have been reported to the help desk. Of course, the client wants problems resolved quickly, but what he really wants is not to have problems to begin with.

Let's assume that if valid statistics were available today, they might show that the client was reporting 50 problems per week, with an average resolution time of 24 hours. If the focus is only on turnaround time, you can imagine, in time, the average response time might be lowered to 12 hours. This would certainly be a better situation for the client. However, if there are still 50 problems reported per week, the client will continue to be dissatisfied.

Likewise, if the help desk and IT support teams are courteous and professional, they would both be ranked highly in those client satisfaction metrics. If, however, the plant continues to report 50 problems per week, will the plant staff really be more satisfied? Probably not.

From the client's perspective, other metrics should be gathered that will help analyze the problems—not just the problem response. Some examples include:

- The number of problems reported per day and per week.
- The number of problems identical to problems previously reported.
- The types of problems grouped into categories, for further root cause or Pareto analysis.
- The severity of the problems (focus on eliminating major problems, then medium, then minor).
- The impact of the problems, in terms of lost hours.

My advice to Terri and Sarah is to keep the metrics they are proposing to collect, but also to talk to the three groups about adding more metrics that get to causes and impacts. There is an old saying, "What gets measured gets done." If Terri and Sarah focus exclusively on the response times, the tendency will be for everyone to focus exclusively in that area. Although important, their goal should be to reduce the number of problems, the severity of the problems, and the impact of the problems to the client. These goals will require different metrics.

Evaluate All Risk Response Options in the Risk Plan

A cold chill was starting to blow into Dickens; the fall season was starting to take shape. The leaves on the oak trees outside my office window were beginning to turn orange and red. Short-sleeve shirts were being replaced by light turtlenecks and long-sleeve sweaters. The NFL was already in its third week. Pam was starting to wonder what costume to buy Tim for Halloween. It was just the third week of September, but people's minds were starting to turn to thoughts of Thanksgiving, Christmas, and winter. John Santos was no exception. He asked me to come by his office on Wednesday afternoon around 3 p.m. to provide final feedback on his project charter.

"Tom, I can't believe I saw a store putting up Christmas decorations last night. I tell you, Christmas comes earlier and earlier every year," he said with a chuckle as I came into his office.

I pulled out my iPad and pretended to look busy for a few moments. "Actually, it says here Christmas is December 25th again this year," I replied with a straight face. After a few seconds I smiled and we both laughed. We talked for a few more minutes about gift ideas for our kids before discussing work.

John's project charter was, all in all, a pretty good document, although I did want to talk to him about his risk plan. He was responsible for a project involving a major office move at our headquarters. A couple of business units had recently reorganized, and the inevitable follow-up had people moving to different offices and floors to reflect the new organization charts.

"John, I see you have identified a number of risks to the project," I noted. "For each risk, you have also identified a plan to try to eliminate it. However, the move is not for three months. Given the timeline, I wonder whether there might be more sensible alternatives to some of your risk plans."

"There are a number of potential risks with a project this large," John replied. "The moving logistics are complex, and everything needs to happen in a sequence. If one move gets delayed, the entire schedule gets pushed back."

"I understand how interdependent everything is," I sympathized. "However, let's look at some of the risk plans. For instance, your moving company may end up on strike, so you are proposing engaging another company instead. This is a new company you have not used before."

"Yes," John agreed. "If our standard moving contractor is on strike, we need to have an alternative in place."

"You are also planning for a high volume of calls from people who need some minor tweaking after the move," I noted. "You plan to have your staff work paid overtime on nights and weekends to deal with this demand."

John spoke proudly. "This may cost us a bunch of overtime pay, but we are going to keep our service level up by responding to all requests within 48 hours."

"I see where you're going with your risk plans," I summed up. "However, there are a number of responses to perceived risks. You are trying to mitigate, or eliminate each risk. Let's discuss some alternatives and see if they are applicable instead."

LESSON

Since risks are generally perceived as bad, it makes sense that the first instinct of a project manager would be to eliminate them. Mitigation is a risk response that tries to minimize the probability of a risk occurring (down to 0 percent, which would eliminate it entirely) or to minimize the impact of the risk on your project (down to zero impact, which would make the risk irrelevant). However, there are a number of other options for responding to a risk, including:

- **Leave it**: This option is appropriate if you recognize the risk but don't have any practical way to deal with it. This is also a good option if the cost of managing the risk is greater than the risk impact on your project.
- **Monitor the risk**: This is a good option if the risk event is quite a ways in the future. You may have enough time to monitor the risk to see if it will go away on its own. The project manager can create a risk plan later when the risk event is closer if the probability and impact of the risk are still too high.
- **Avoid the risk**: You may be able to isolate and avoid the condition causing the risk. For instance, if there is risk associated with a new model of equipment, you may decide to use the older equipment model. In this case, the entire risk was avoided by changing the nature of the project.
- **Move the risk**: In some instances, the responsibility for managing a risk can be removed from the project by assigning the risk to another entity or third party. For example, you may have risk associated with the lack of a key skill in your organization. You may outsource this work to a third party. The risk is still there but it is now the responsibility of the third party.

Notice that none of these options include ignoring the risk. Even the option to leave the risk is the result of a conscious decision.

In John's case, he is choosing to mitigate all of the identified risks. However, I asked him to be open to other options as well. For instance, let's look at the risk of a strike at the moving contractor. John has three months until the move. Perhaps he should not make any major changes now, such as developing a business relationship with a new company. Perhaps the best approach is to monitor this risk for the next 30 days. If the labor contract is renewed, he won't need to make any changes at all. If a strike still seems imminent, then he'll still have two months to put new plans into place. There is also risk associated with using a new vendor on an important move like this. John probably doesn't want to change moving contractors unless absolutely necessary.

John is also proposing heavy overtime so his service level will not drop after the move is complete. This may be the best approach, but has he looked at alternatives? He should talk to his manager and major clients about another option—leaving the risk alone. After a major move, people understand there is going to be some disruption in service levels. He may be able to reset expectations for a short-term time frame. For instance, perhaps turnaround time for problems will be five days instead of two days. This may be a situation the company can live with and may not require him to incur the expense of paid overtime.

John's risk plan is not wrong. In fact, these may be the best alternatives given what he knows today. However, a number of options are available for risk response. In general, risk response is based on the probability of the risk occurring, the impact to the project, and other factors such as the time frame when the risk event may occur. The project manager should look at all the appropriate risk response options, and the risk plan should be evaluated periodically to ensure it continue to address each risk appropriately.

Manage Client Expectations

My workload was unusually slow during the last week of September, so
I decided to proactively check in with several project managers to see if
I could offer any assistance. My first meeting was with Nikki Hooper;
she was working with her client to update an application on how com-
missions were paid. Nikki was a mother of three with short blonde hair
and green eyes. An extremely conservative woman, Nikki was active on
her church board as well as her school's Parent Teacher Association.
This was my first interaction with her, and I could tell she was skeptical
about whether I could offer any real advice or help. Like many people I
had worked with in my role as project management advisor, she also
appeared nervous, thinking that my true function was to assess her performance and competence as a project manager and to determine
whether she was someone worth keeping at Mega Manufacturing. I addressed this misconception first.

"You know, Nikki, a lot of people think my job is to evaluate project
managers," I began. "This could not be further from the truth. I was
brought in to help project managers like you do their job more professionally and more effectively."

"Thanks for saying that up front, Tom," she replied. "I was a bit nervous after receiving your call because I thought perhaps you had heard something bad about my project. I actually thought my client might have called to complain."

"Not at all. But why is your client complaining? Why don't you fill me in and let's see if I can help."

"Well, I am really having a problem right now trying to manage client expectations," she began. "Our business clients aren't being realistic. They want to completely automate the commission payment process and allow the salespeople to view information through the Web. We can't do everything they want because we are dealing with enhancements to a legacy system with a lot of older technology. We would have to completely rewrite it if we did everything they want. I would love to hear your advice on how to better manage their expectations."

"Managing expectations can be tough," I replied, still trying to put her at ease. "But the place to start is the project charter. Did you write one for this project?"

"No, we didn't," she said. "We didn't think we needed one for an enhancement."

"How about business requirements?" I asked. "Do you have anything formally approved coming out of your analysis?"

"We met with the clients to gather their requirements, but we don't have much formally documented."

I paused for a few seconds. "Well, you asked me for advice on how to better manage the expectations of your client," I said. "The problem is you and your client never had an agreement on what your project was going to produce. You can't manage expectations effectively unless you have common expectations to begin with."

LESSON

Managing expectations is one of the biggest challenges facing project managers. It seems as if your client always wants more than you can deliver—for less cost and effort than it really takes. This mismatch of expectations is one of the primary reasons projects don't end successfully. In many cases, the project team has one level of expectations for what the project will produce, but the sponsor and clients have another. The challenge for the project manager is to keep the project team expectations synchronized with the major stakeholders.

If you were to create a process for managing client expectations on a project, it would look something like this:

- **Establish an agreement**: This is probably the most overlooked yet obvious part of the process. It is difficult or impossible to manage client expectations if you don't have an agreement to begin with. The agreement should be with the sponsor. For instance, this happens with the sponsor approval of the Project Charter and business requirements.

- **Manage change**: Once an agreement is reached, changes should be managed through the change management process. This ensures the sponsor approves all changes and helps to keep expectations in line.

- **Deliver against the expectations**: Again, this may seem obvious. However, once an agreement is reached, you need to make sure you deliver the work as expected.

- **Communicate proactively**: Communicate proactively through the status reporting process or as part of a broader Communication Plan. This helps the sponsor and stakeholders keep up to date on progress, issues, risks, etc.

- **Periodically assess performance**: The project manager needs to monitor the work to ensure that the client commitments are met. If there is a drift from the prior commitments, the project manager needs to do everything in his power to get back within expectations.

- **Reset expectations if necessary**: If the project manager feels the team is unlikely to meet the expectations, immediate steps should be taken to determine a new course of action and reset expectations with a modified agreement.

- **Complete the agreement**: Review the completed work with the client to ensure the terms of the agreement have been fully met. If not, negotiate what will be required to fulfill the agreement.

It's no wonder Nikki is having trouble keeping client expectations in line with hers. After all, she never had a formal agreement with the client on the definition of the work (scope, objectives, risk, deliverables, etc.) to begin with. Nor did she set a common expectation as to the features and functions that would be delivered (business requirements). It's not surprising, then, that the client has "unrealistic" expectations as to what will be delivered.

Nikki won't be able to manage expectations effectively until she gains a common understanding of the work with her client. Since the project is well underway, it's probably too late to go all the way back to the Project Charter. However, she can go back and document the business requirements. Once the requirements are on the table, she can provide effort and cost estimates. When the sponsor sees that some of the requirements are prohibitively expensive to implement, he or she should agree to concentrate on those areas of the project that offer reasonable and cost-effective delivery. Until then, Nikki will always have a hard time managing the work because she has no agreement on what will be delivered.

Use Milestones to Track Overall Progress

The first week of October brought cold winds and rain to Dickens—as well as numerous calls and e-mails for project management advice. I knew the next few months leading up to the end of the year would be busy as my calendar was filling up fast.

I had just returned from a set of back-to-back-to-back-to-back meetings when I received a panicked phone call from Jerry asking me if I could spare 20 minutes to swing by the large conference room on the third floor at the end of the day. It required rescheduling a late meeting with Alex, but I told Jerry I could make it.

As I approached the conference room at 5 p.m., I saw Jerry outside the main door.

"Hey, Jerry. What's up?" I asked.

"Tom, I know you hate surprises, but happy birthday!"

Just then the conference room door swung open to reveal several people in birthday hats and a big cake on the conference table. I wasn't sure if anyone knew it was my 40th birthday, but apparently the word had gotten out. Mega Manufacturing is a big company, so birthdays are traditionally celebrated internally by team members. Since I was really just a team of one, I assumed I wouldn't be having a birthday celebration. It was nice to know that people remembered me. I blew out the candles on the cake and grabbed the first piece.

After several minutes of socializing, I noticed Alex in the back corner eating a piece of cake. I went over to see him.

"Hey Alex! I feel bad about canceling our appointment for a social function. I honestly thought Jerry was in trouble on his project."

"No need to explain, Tom. Jerry called me early this morning and let me in on the secret. If you don't mind, perhaps we can still talk briefly about my project. I could use your help with something."

"Why don't you update me on your project? How's it going?"

"Well, I think we are in pretty good shape," he said. "We have a number of changes to make to the database environment, but the work is not necessarily complex. It's just that we have a couple hundred databases to upgrade and it takes time."

"It sounds like a challenge," I agreed. "You said you thought you were in good shape. Does that mean you are on schedule or ahead of schedule?"

"I think we are on target," he said with a slight hesitation. "But, to be honest, I would have a hard time telling you precisely. We have many of our database administrators working on this project full time or part time. If one of them has some free time, they are jumping ahead to the next database upgrade. If other problems come up, they may not work on the upgrade for a number of days. So, some of them are ahead of schedule and some are behind. It's hard to figure out exactly where we are at any single point in time."

We talked for a few minutes about how he was tracking accomplishments. I didn't have a major concern with how Alex was running the project, but I thought it was a problem that he was unable to note exactly where he stood against his schedule.

"Let's talk some more about your schedule" I said to Alex. "It seems like you have planned the project well, and it appears you are assigning work effectively. I think you need to set up some schedule milestones so you can better judge how your project is doing against your plan."

LESSON

Milestones are inserted into the schedule to signify the completion of a major deliverable or a major set of deliverables. They have zero duration. That is, they do not specifically require any work or effort to complete. However, they signify that the project has completed some piece of work.

Milestones are especially of interest to managers and sponsors because they can provide a high-level snapshot of how you are tracking against your project schedule. For instance, you may add a milestone at the end of the analysis phase. Your sponsor and other stakeholders can track the status of the project against the milestone date without needing to understand the more detailed activities. So if the analysis phase milestone is missed, they will know that the work leading up to that milestone was not completed on time. They don't need to know the details. They can tell the project is trending behind schedule. On the other hand, if you hit your milestone date, the assumption is the work is on track from a schedule perspective.

Milestones also provide the opportunity for a project management checkpoint. At every milestone, project managers can do the following:

- Evaluate previously identified risks to ensure they are being managed well.
- Look for new risks to the project.
- Verify that they have business commitment to continue.
- Check whether project assumptions are still valid.
- Double-check the budget and deadline estimates to determine if they are still achievable.

After validating that the prior work is complete and the project is ready to proceed, you can plunge ahead with the next major part of the project.

Usually when you are managing a project, many (or most) of the activities follow a sequential pattern. For example, major analysis is followed by design, which is typically followed by construction. In most cases, the project manager can insert a milestone at the end of each of these project phases. However, on Alex's project, the activities are scheduled more arbitrarily and so don't necessarily follow a logical pattern. The timing of the work is based as much on team member availability as anything else.

In spite of the scheduling difficulty, or perhaps because of it, Alex needs some milestones to gauge his progress. For example, he could set up milestones at the completion of the database upgrades for each business unit or after every 25 databases are converted.

The funny thing about Alex's project is that he has done a very good job of building his schedule and is managing it well. In spite of this, he is nervous about whether he really understands if he is ahead of or behind schedule. This is always a cause for concern because project managers should always know how they are trending against their schedules. If they don't, there is a good chance they could be behind schedule and not realize it until too late. Establishing milestones will allow Alex to focus on how the work is progressing.

In a simplistic sense, when a milestone arrives, Alex can see whether all the work up to that point is complete. If it is, he is on or ahead of schedule. If some work is ahead of schedule and some behind schedule (which sounds like what is happening on Alex's project), he can shift available resources to overdue work so the project can catch up with the planned schedule. At that point, he can confirm that all the work required up to that milestone is completed. He should also have some sense of whether the project is ahead of or behind schedule based on knowing the date the milestone was scheduled to be completed, the date it actually was completed, and the amount of work (if any) that has been completed ahead of schedule based on the milestone date.

Establishing milestones will provide Alex with checkpoints he can use to validate whether his project is progressing well against the schedule or whether corrective action is required.

Catch Errors as Early as Possible

Sean Robinson scheduled another meeting with me for the second week of October, and I was curious to see how he was doing on his project to track response rates for direct mail campaigns. The last time I saw him was in the parking lot after work as he was heading to the gym. When I saw him this morning in his office, it was clear he had just come from the gym—his gym bag was on the floor next to his desk and he had that "just showered" look. I didn't know much about Sean, but I knew he took his physical well-being very seriously.

"How many times do you work out a day, Sean?" I asked in a teasing tone as I put my coffee mug down on the corner of his desk.

"Usually just once—either in the morning or after work. If I'm really motivated, I go both times!"

"Wow, that sounds pretty intense. I'm lucky to get in one workout every other day."

"Well, it just takes discipline, Tom. I'd be happy to meet you in the gym every day, either before or after work. We can work out together, and I'll get you started on a diet and exercise program that will make you feel great!"

I knew I was getting in over my head. "I'm not sure I can commit the time right now, but I'll get back to you on it," I replied, trying not to sound too uninterested. "Tell you what, let's exercise our brains a bit this morning."

We both chuckled. We last spoke a month or two ago, so if Sean was on track, his project should be winding down about now.

"We're getting to the end," Sean said, shifting his weight. "But the user acceptance testing is taking longer than expected. I guess that's good and bad. It's bad that it is taking more time than expected, but on the positive side, the more errors we catch in testing, the higher the quality of the final solution."

Sean's mention of the "higher quality of the final solution" intrigued me.

"What kind of errors are you catching?" I asked.

"Our users are being very thorough—they are catching all kinds of errors. Most are in the interfaces between the various subsystems. Some are programming logic errors. A couple of the worst problems were caused by some screw-ups in the original requirements. Those have taken quite a bit of time to correct." Sean began stretching his legs.

"It's great that your users are catching all these errors. But did you perform any quality reviews or get any user signoffs on your work as it was originally being completed?"

"No, we didn't," Sean said, chuckling. "We probably should have done more things like that. But it seemed like we didn't have the time."

"It seems like you do have the time," I countered. "You're just spending it now instead of earlier in the project. In fact, I'll bet you are spending more time fixing problems now than you would have spent avoiding them earlier."

LESSON

Everyone has heard the sarcastic saying, "You don't have time to do it right, but you do have time to do it twice." This means the incremental time required to validate that the work is done correctly the first time is sacrificed, and you are then forced to spend extra time on rework and fixing problems at the end of the project. In many cases, your familiarity with the project lifecycle has reached the point where you think you can rush through many activities in the project. There is a sense that you can get everything right the first time. Unfortunately, it doesn't usually happen. The errors are discovered. It is just that they are discovered later in the project instead of earlier.

There are two main philosophies behind project quality management: define good work processes that reduce the number of errors to begin with, and find leftover errors as early as possible after they are introduced.

The first aspect of building better processes involves activities like training, checklists for processes, following standard policies, and process improvement. These are all investments in helping the team members create deliverables correctly the first time. These types of activities are known as quality assurance, and this work focuses on preventing errors in the first place. If you train your team, for instance, in how to apply a new technology, the team should be able to use the new technology correctly and with a minimum of errors.

The second aspect of finding errors as early as possible includes activities like inspections, signoffs, and walkthroughs. For instance, misunderstandings and mistakes in deliverable definitions need to be discovered in the planning process. One way to avoid misunderstandings is to make sure the sponsor signs and approves the Project Charter. Likewise, errors in business logic need to be caught in the business requirements phase. Design errors need to be caught in the design phase, and errors in constructing a solution need to be identified when the solution is constructed. This work is referred to as quality control and it requires some form of inspection to find errors in the solution after the fact.

The project manager should be aware that, in almost all cases, a good quality management process requires more effort hours and cost at the beginning of the project. However, these costs are more than offset by a reduction in the time needed to correct errors later in the project, or worse, when the solution goes live.

The fact that Sean is catching so many errors at the end of the project is not a sign of a good quality solution. In fact, it may be an indicator of a lack of quality in the process used to build the solution. It would have been much less costly for Sean's team to have spotted problems with the business requirements during the analysis phase of the project, rather than having to fix the problems during user acceptance testing. These errors in requirements could have been uncovered simply by having the client formally approve the requirements. This is not to say the requirements would have then been perfect. It is always possible the client may have missed some of the important requirements needed for the project. However, having to formally approve the requirements would have forced the client to review this information more diligently. It would also have allowed Sean to invoke scope change management when new requirements came up late in the project.

The other errors Sean mentions have to do with the testing process. The purpose of the client acceptance test is simply to validate that the solution works as expected. This is not the time to be catching interface errors and programming errors. Based on the fact that his users are finding these types of errors, it appears that both the programming process and the subsequent testing process had flaws. These types of errors should have been caught earlier and are a sign that the testing process was not rigorous enough.

Gain Sponsor Approval for Scope Changes Requiring Budget and Deadline Deviation

Mega Manufacturing offered its employees many great perks, but the one I enjoyed most was the cafeteria. The company contracted a catering firm in Chicago called Cool Eats to run the cafeteria, and the selection was stupendous. Every day you could pick items from a vast salad bar, deli, Chinese wok, American grill, and fruit stand. There was also an ice cream bar, which I didn't visit frequently—but every now and again it hit the spot. Usually, the pressures of work meant that I just grabbed a quick snack at my desk, but I would like to eat in the cafeteria more often. Today I was doing just that. I was having lunch with Danielle Bartlett. I brought my cheeseburger and fries over to a table and Danielle joined me.

Danielle was finishing up her second project since I first met her on Valentine's Day. Her latest project was to establish an intranet portal web site that could be used to communicate more effectively between the Facilities Department and its numerous vendors.

"Looks good," Danielle said, eyeing my burger and fries as she set her tray down. "Let me grab a soda and I'll be right back." Danielle had ordered a small salad and chicken soup, so I knew she must either be eating healthy or calming her stomach.

"Danielle, your lunch suggests your stomach might be bothering you. Are you stressed out about something?"

"You are very wise, Tom," she said with a smile. She said her project was going over budget and past its estimated end date. Her sponsor had just found out and was not happy.

"Frankly, I am a little surprised," she began, sipping her soup. "I thought I was managing the project well. We developed a set of requirements for the installation of the estimating package, but as the project progressed, the users had new requirements they had forgotten to include in the initial stages of analysis. Whenever this happened, I initiated standard scope change management procedures."

"Tell me what your scope change procedures were," I replied. "Perhaps they were missing some important piece."

Danielle described the process to me. "Whenever a scope change request was made, we documented it and created a cost estimate. Then we took the change to the client and verified whether the business benefit of the change was worth the cost and effort. If she said to go ahead, we proceeded. In fact, I have everything documented."

"You'll need to explain to me why your sponsor is unhappy," I said. "If you invoked scope change management, and the change was approved, the impact to the project should have been known."

"The sponsor says she didn't approve the changes and she was not aware that the project was going over budget," she replied. "I guess we didn't do a good enough job of managing her expectations."

Now I was really confused. "I don't understand. I thought you said the sponsor approved all the scope changes?"

"No, I said the client approved the changes," she explained. "When a user requested a change, we always went to their manager for approval. I thought if a manager approved the work, we should go ahead."

"Now I see," I concluded. "You have made the common mistake of not understanding the full role of the sponsor. There may be many people who are users and stakeholders, but the only person who can approve a scope change is the sponsor."

"I guess that makes sense," she said, finishing her soup.

"You know, Danielle, my mom always used to say that ice cream is good for settling your stomach. How about I buy you a scoop?"

"You read my mind again," she replied. "My mom says that ice cream is good for the soul. We definitely need to heed our mothers' advice today!"

LESSON

There are many people who have an interest in your project. The clients are the people or the organization(s) that receive the benefits delivered by the project. These people or organizations may also be called customers. The end users are the people in the client organization who will actually use the products produced from the project. Not all projects have end users. There are also many other stakeholders who have an interest in your project but don't specifically belong to the client organization. And, of course, there is the sponsor. The sponsor is the specific person that owns the project and obtained the project funding.

It is natural for the project team to want to please their clients. However, this desire to be "client focused" often leads them to forget the main client of the project. The team most often works with the end users and their managers. The end users and their managers are typically the people who provide requirements, answer questions, and validate that the solution is complete and correct. The end users are the people who will ultimately live with the final solution. Since these are the people the project team deals with the most, they are often considered to be the ultimate client. However, they are really the "little c" client.

When it comes to declaring success or failure, and when it comes to managing expectations, the sponsor matters most. And when you have to consider changing the budget or delivery date, the sponsor is the person with the power. The sponsor is the "big C" Client.

Danielle thought she had a good scope change management process for her project. She was

1.   Receiving scope change requests from end users;

2.   Documenting the requests;

3.   Estimating the impact of the changes to the project; and

4.   Taking them to the client manager for approval.

In reality, the client manager was just verifying whether the scope change provided a benefit. The client manager was not in a position to decide the business value by comparing the benefit of the change with the impact to the project.

All of this may have slipped through if the project budget and deadline had not been compromised. However, these lower-level managers can't make decisions requiring budget and deadline changes. They don't have authority to add to the project budget. In these instances, only the sponsor can make the decisions. Of course, the sponsor may delegate this role to another person for day-to-day items. In that case, the sponsor designee would be the only one to make these types of decisions.

Danielle and I had a good discussion on this point. She was trying to follow a good scope change process. However, she was not going to the right person to make decisions that had an impact on the budget or deadline. The client manager may have thought the changes were important, but she didn't have the authority to approve additional time or budget. The sponsor was the one to make those decisions. Now Danielle finds herself in an uncomfortable position. In her desire to be client focused, she has upset the client that matters most—the project sponsor.

Be Proactive to Accelerate the Project Schedule

Lindsay Peterson stops by my office on Halloween day to discuss her project to consolidate worldwide sales data for the Sales Department. I hardly recognize her when she steps into my office. She is wearing a white jumpsuit, big gold glasses, and a fake wig. Mega Manufacturing encourages its employees to come dressed in costumes for Halloween, and Lindsay's is one of the best—a female Elvis!

"Boy, it's tough to imagine the teenagers swooning over you," I joke as she comes in and sits down.

"Very funny, Tom. Tell me, who exactly are you supposed to be?"

I am wearing a regular suit and tie, but I have an old reporter's hat on, with glasses and an exaggerated part in my hair. I stand up to provide a clearer clue as to my identity. I have purposely left the middle buttons on my dress shirt undone, and I pull them aside to show Lindsay my blue T-shirt with a large "S" printed on it.

"Ah, Clark Kent. Very clever."

"What do you mean?" I say in a deadpan voice. "I'm not wearing a costume today." We both laugh.

"Tell me, 'King,' what's got you in Heartbreak Hotel on your project?"

"Well, we recently came up with a workaround to replace some web reporting software that wouldn't work with our browser," Lindsay starts. "We are now behind schedule and I want to get some tips from you on things we can do to catch up."

"Have you tried anything so far?" I ask.

"We have assigned a couple of new part-time people to the project," Lindsay notes. "But they aren't having much effect. At this point, we will probably end up missing our deadline. However, I want to prepare a new schedule to see how close we can get to the original date."

"Okay," I agree, standing up to write on the whiteboard. "First, let's verify that your new part-time resources are working on the right activities. Then let's list a number of techniques that will help to accelerate the schedule."

LESSON

The project manager starts off a project with a schedule. However, it seems that projects never behave exactly as planned and soon you need to make adjustments. Some activities end late and new ones come along that you didn't account for. If you're lucky, some activities complete early and there's some built-in contingency to help absorb inaccurate estimates. However, if you are unlucky (and this seems to be the case more often than not) you end up in a situation where you start trending over your deadline.

The project manager must always understand the actual progress of the project compared to the baseline schedule. ("Baseline" refers to the original approved schedule plus any approved changes.) The project manager must also know what still needs to be done to complete the project. This will allow you to catch variances, risks, and problems as early as possible. For example, if you find you are trending four weeks behind schedule, it's better to understand this with six months to go rather than with two months to go. The earlier you recognize the problem, the more flexibility you have to resolve the situation.

If you realize you are trending past your deadline, you must try to understand the cause(s). If you don't understand the cause of the schedule problem, you may put a plan in place that fails because the problem continues to occur. Some project managers realize they are trending over their deadline date and immediately ask for more time. However, this is not the first option. If anything, this should be the last option. Instead, once you understand the cause of the schedule delay, you need to put a plan in place to get back on schedule. If you can't meet your committed deadline, you should strive to complete the work as close to the original deadline as possible.

The following list contains examples of techniques that can be applied to get back on schedule. This list is not in order of priority. Many of the techniques will be viable in certain situations. A project manager should be familiar with many schedule management techniques so that he can apply the best techniques based on the situation and the cause of the problem. Some of these techniques may require additional funding, but that may be a viable option if the deadline date is more important than the budget.

- **Work overtime**: Everyone hates it, but one way to get back on schedule is overtime. If people work more hours, they can get more work done in the same amount of calendar time. Overtime may be the best option if you are close to the end of the project and just need a final push to get everything done on schedule (tip: consider giving people time off after the project is completed). If you are still early in the project, there are probably other options that are more effective. Note that there may be cost implications to this option if you need to have contract resources or other chargeable team members work overtime.

- **Reallocate resources onto the critical path**: The project manager must understand the activities on the critical path. After all, if the project is trending over deadline, by definition the critical path is late. Once the critical path is understood, you should see if resources can be moved from other activities to help the activities on the critical path. It is possible that re-allocating people within the team may cause their original activities to be delayed. However, since these activities are off the critical path, they will have some slack. Remember, the activities on the critical path are key. You may have the option to assign a more productive resource to the critical path activities, while reassigning a less-productive resource to non-critical path activities. Be careful though—delaying some work off the critical path may end up changing the critical path. Always double-check the critical path each time you change the schedule.

Lindsay should explore this option in more detail. She has applied two part-time resources to the project with minimal results. It's possible they were assigned activities off the critical path. It is also possible they worked on the critical path, but as the path was shortened, a new critical path emerged.

- **Double-check all dependencies**: Schedule dependencies represent activities that must be executed in a certain order. Invalid dependencies make it appear activities must be performed sequentially, when they can really be done in parallel. For instance, if you are building a house, you can't start putting up the frame until the foundation is poured and dried. If you are trending over your deadline, these dependencies should be revalidated, since it is possible the schedule is being lengthened by unnecessary dependencies between activities.

- **Check time-constrained activities**: Time-constrained activities don't change based on the number of resources applied. For instance, you may be assigning team members to a five-day class. The class takes five days if one person attends, and it takes five days if 20 people attend. All of these time-constrained activities should be checked to verify the timeframe. Perhaps the time-constrained activity could be shortened with a different approach.

- **Swap resources**: One cause for trending over your deadline might be that one or more resources are not as productive as you originally planned. In some instances, you may need to release a team member and bring in another person. For example, you may have been assigned the best team members available when your project started. However, later in the project other potential team members may be available and you may want to swap a weak team member with one that is more productive.

- **"Crash" the schedule**: *Crashing the schedule* means applying additional resources to the critical path to get the biggest schedule gain for the least amount of incremental costs. For instance, let's assume one person was assigned to complete an activity in ten days. If two people can complete the work in six days, you will have accelerated the schedule by four days at an incremental cost of two work days (two people for six days versus the original ten-day estimate). You may be able to further crash the schedule by applying three resources; perhaps now the activity would take four days. Typically, the more resources you throw at an activity, the higher the incremental cost, while you will receive less in incremental time savings. If you are crashing the schedule, you are willing to make this trade-off of schedule compression versus additional project costs.

- **Fast track**: *Fast track* means you look at activities normally done in sequence and instead schedule them partially in parallel. For instance, in the home building example, the house frame couldn't be constructed until the foundation was dry. However, if the house is large enough, you may have options to fast track by starting to erect the frame on the side of the home where the foundation was poured first. The foundation will harden there first and might allow you to erect the frame on that side while the foundation on the far side of the home is still drying. Fast-tracking always increases the risk of having to do some re-work later. If there was no risk of re-work, the activities should always have been scheduled with some overlap.

- **"Zero tolerance" scope change**: Many projects begin to trend over deadline because more work has been added than originally committed to. This could be a result of poor scope change management, or it could be that small changes are being added without proper scope change management. (These small scope changes are sometimes referred to as "scope creep.") However, if you are at risk of missing your deadline date, you must work with the client and team members to ensure absolutely no unplanned work is being requested or worked on—even if it is just one hour—without going through formal scope change management processes.

- **Improve processes**: Sometimes a schedule can be accelerated by improving internal project work processes. You should solicit team member feedback and look for ways to streamline processes. For instance, perhaps you have a daily status meeting that doesn't provide value and can be scaled back to once per week. You may also find there are bottlenecks with getting deliverables approved that can be removed through a more streamlined process.

- **Improve morale**: Sometimes poor morale causes deadline dates to drift. If poor morale is one of the reasons you are having schedule problems, you can spend time trying to improve it. Team members will work harder and perform better if they don't spend time complaining and sulking. You can build shared purpose, increase camaraderie, and do some fun things to get people excited and happy again.

- **Scope back the work**: One of the last options to consider is to look at the work remaining and negotiate with the sponsor to remove some of it from the project. If some of the remaining work is not essential to the project, you could discuss eliminating it completely. You may also have some options to complete this project on time with less than 100 percent functionality, and then execute a follow-up project to complete the remaining requirements.

It will take a discussion between Lindsay and her sponsor to determine which options are best for their project. If the deadline date is important, the worst thing a project manager can do is ignore the schedule overrun and just let things keep going as they are. There are many proactive techniques that can be applied to accelerate the schedule. Lindsay can have an intelligent discussion with the sponsor to look at the alternatives, how much each option will accelerate the schedule, and the incremental cost to the project (if any).

Use the Work Breakdown Structure to Identify All the Work

Pam and I took Tim trick-or-treating on Halloween night until about 9:30 p.m. He picked out his own costume this year, settling on Buzz Lightyear from the Toy Story movies. His pumpkin-shaped bucket was nearly full when we get home, but he was so tired from walking around and carrying his bounty he quickly fell asleep on the couch. I recounted the story of our night to Marty McKnight in her office the following afternoon, and she laughed when I told her about Tim falling asleep right away. Apparently her youngest daughter did the same thing.

"She enjoyed getting all dressed up as a ballerina, but she didn't particularly care for ringing doorbells and asking strangers for candy. By the time we got home, she could barely keep her eyes open," she said. Marty was in her late 20s and had only a few years' experience in the Marketing department of Mega Manufacturing.

"I don't know if you feel the same, but for me the best part of trick-or-treating with Tim is all the free candy for dad!" I said with a smirk.

"Oh that's definitely my reward as well. My daughter Emelia loves Tootsie Rolls, so I immediately put all those aside for her, but then I admit I indulged in a few peanut butter cups. I used to love those when I was a kid!"

"I like those as well. Anything with chocolate is my favorite!" I said before taking my seat around Marty's work table.

"Why don't you bring me up to speed on your project, Marty?" I asked.

"I'm an analyst in the Marketing Department," Marty began. "As you know, we have been doing marketing campaigns for many years, and some are very successful. However, we have a new department head, and he wants us to revamp the traditional model we have for campaigns. He wants them to be developed sooner, include a social media component, appeal to younger customers, and be backed up with more metrics that show their effectiveness. He wants more changes as well, but you get the picture."

"Loud and clear," I said. "It sounds like he wants to reengineer your overall model for conducting marketing campaigns."

"Yes, that's the word he used—'reengineering,'" Marty confirmed "So, I figured 'reengineering' is an IT term, right? That's why I asked you to come over today. I thought you could give me some advice for how to put a game plan together. I'm not really sure how to begin."

"Well, 'reengineering' is not really an IT term," I noted, trying to sound competent without sounding too smart. "In fact, much of the common use of the term is in the context of business reengineering, which is exactly what you are trying to do. I have a technique to get you started on a new model. It's called a Work Breakdown Structure."

LESSON

What is Marty looking for? She has been asked to build a model that will describe how the Marketing Department will conduct campaigns in the future. This model is basically a schedule template. The model will describe what things you do to start a campaign, determine the audience, work with vendors, analyze the market, gather metrics, etc. You can easily see that the result of Marty's effort will be a schedule template describing all of the activities required to create, launch, and track a marketing campaign.

What's unusual about her project is that she has been asked only to create the schedule model. In most cases, you build your schedule and then use it to execute a project. Marty is building a schedule template for other marketing teams to use after her.

One of the ways to begin building a schedule is with a technique called *Work Breakdown Structure (WBS)*. The WBS technique is especially helpful when you are unsure what you are getting into. It is possible one person could create the WBS; however, that would imply one person has all the knowledge, which is typically not the case.

The place to start is to gather a group of people with knowledge and expertise in this area. The meeting can be facilitated, but it doesn't have to be. The session rarely starts with a blank slate. There is usually some pre-existing information—such as goals, strategies, constraints, and standards—that help to frame the overall solution. If you have a Project Charter, be sure to note the deliverables, assumptions, approach, etc. In Marty's case, for instance, the group can start by listing the stated requirements from the sponsor, such as including the web components, appealing to younger customers, and executing faster.

With a WBS technique, you first determine the large chunks of work that must be carried out for the entire project to be completed. At this point, how you define the first level of work doesn't matter. It is only important for all of the work to be identified at the end of the process. For instance, a marketing campaign might be initially broken up into major phases such as planning, analysis, design, build, and rollout. Another common way to start the WBS is by identifying the major deliverables such as television, radio, magazine, newspaper, social media, and point-of-sale. If this was an IT application, the deliverables might be an online application, data warehouse, datamart, and user query tools. If these are large deliverables, you can break them down further into sub-deliverables (also called *work packages*). The initial high-level breakdown of work is called level 1.

It is possible that your WBS could stop after identifying all of the deliverables and work packages. This would be referred to as a *deliverable-based WBS*. However, you can also break the work down further to the activity level. This work goes on the WBS as well. These activities can, in turn, be broken down even further into smaller activities. The work can continue to be broken down further if it is not clear what is required to complete the work or if the estimate to complete the work is less than an estimating threshold—usually around 80 hours (this threshold could be larger for larger projects). This could take you down to three, four, or five levels of ever more detailed activities. It's rare that you need to break the work down more than five levels.

Once the WBS is complete you can estimate the effort to complete the lowest level of work, sequence the activities, assign resources, estimate duration, and estimate costs. The end result of this process is the creation of a project schedule. In Marty's case, she will have a schedule template of what it takes to execute a marketing campaign. The WBS is not the same as a schedule, but it is usually the starting point to create the schedule.

My advice to Marty is to get a team of marketing people together and build a WBS that lays out the work they think should be done on future campaigns. The group can estimate and sequence the work to determine the order and dependencies. They can assign generic roles to the work based on the type of person that would normally perform the activity. The generic roles will suffice since they are creating a schedule template, not a specific schedule for a specific project.

When a marketing campaign starts in the future, the campaign manager will use the generic schedule as the model. The campaign manager can remove unnecessary activities, assign resources to the remaining activities, and estimate the effort and duration of each activity. The marketing campaign plan can then be executed. This generic schedule template will ensure that each marketing campaign is carried out in a similar manner, and it will save the campaign manager the time of having to build the work schedule from scratch each time.

Write Your Status Reports from the Reader's Perspective

When Wayne Moretti left Mega Manufacturing, I began reporting to Rick Goodall, a senior vice president. Rick was a great guy who fully supported the idea of a project management adviser and really saw the value of the position. He took me to lunch the day before Wayne left, and we've had a good working relationship ever since. He invited me to lunch the week of Thanksgiving to discuss status reports and to catch up on other business.

We decided to walk to Joe's Fishmarket, a new restaurant about two blocks west of Mega Manufacturing. I knew it opened a few weeks ago, but I didn't know anyone who had eaten there. I ordered the fish 'n' chips special and Rick tried the flounder. We started off talking about nonbusiness-related matters. As our lunch arrived, though, Rick passed along some feedback about status reporting.

"Tom, I've been hearing concerns from some of the senior managers about the quality of the information being reported in the project status reports," Rick said between bites of his french fries. "I need you to work with the project managers to make these more effective."

"What kinds of concerns are you hearing?" I asked.

"Some of the managers are receiving project status reports on a monthly basis," Rick explained. "However, these are just a bunch of words. After reading the reports, they still don't have a good under-standing of the project status."

"Our company needs to move to a higher level on status reporting," I agreed. "A year ago, status reports were created sporadically, and eve-ryone used a different format. Now every project manager does status reporting on a monthly basis in a consistent format. However, I agree that the information in the reports is not always at the high-quality level we need it to be."

"Great," Rick replied. "Let's figure out how to get the content improved over the next two monthly reporting cycles. By the way, how's your fish?"

"You know," I sighed. "The fish is a little stale and a little bland."

"Sounds like our status reports!" Rick quipped.

We both chuckled.

LESSON

Is there a project manager who likes to write status reports? If so, I would like to shake his or her hand. It's not uncommon for your team to accomplish great feats, solve perplexing problems, and strive to meet deadlines. Then, when the time comes to tell your managers and your clients about the status of the project, you spend as little time as possible providing the absolute minimum amount of information required. It might be understandable (but still not right) if the project was in trouble. But even project teams doing well don't always communicate effectively in the status report.

Of course, let's also agree that management stakeholders and project sponsors need to be more involved in a project than just spending a few minutes a month reading a status report. If they don't feel that they are getting the information they need, they can always pick up the phone (or even talk face to face) to get more information from the project manager. But project managers need to make life easier for the stakeholders and sponsors.

Project managers must understand that communicating status is one of their fundamental responsibilities. It is the minimum expectation. Communicating status is a way to manage expectations and to keep everyone informed on how the project is progressing. Your managers and stakeholders are working on many projects at any given time. The status report is one way they can keep an eye on your project and know if they need to become more engaged.

The bottom line is the project manager must write the status report to meet the needs of the reader. The reader doesn't want to know all of the details of your project. The reader also doesn't want to read about how smoothly the project is progressing if, in fact, there are problems. Borrowing a phrase from the legal profession, the status report should tell the truth, the whole truth, and nothing but the truth. A good status report should include the following:

- **Project recap**: This is usually in the form of a short opening paragraph that gives an overall summary of how the project is progressing. Sometimes this recap is designed as a series of standard questions such as:

  - Will the project be completed by its deadline date?
  - Will the project meet budget expectations?
  - Are there any major scope change requests?
  - Are there significant new risks?
  - Are issues being addressed and resolved in a timely manner?

  The answers to these types of opening questions provide a quick indication to the reader of whether there are problems with the project. If everything is going well, no further explanation is required. However, if there are problems, or if there are significant variations the reader should know about, they should be described next. For instance, if major change requests were approved, they should be noted here. If the project is behind schedule, this should be noted, as well as what is being done to get back on schedule. This recap section may be the most important section since it provides the overview of the project. You want your readers to read the entire status report. However, if they only read the recap section, they should still understand the overall status of the project. It is very common to include a color indicator that recaps the overall status. Green would indicate that everything is fine. Yellow would point out that caution is required and that the project is at risk of missing its deadline or budget. A red indicator would mean that the project is already in trouble and will miss its budget, deadline, or both.

- **Major accomplishments**: This section provides insight into the significant work accomplishments from the prior reporting period. This is where the project manager must be careful to communicate in a manner the reader will understand. This section can't be too technical, nor should it be so high level the reader has no perspective on what the accomplishments mean.

- **Major work planned for next period**: This is similar to the prior section, but it gives the reader a sense for the work coming up. Again, communicate this in a way that the reader will understand.

- **Other information**: Other information important to the organization may be included here; for example, this could be other sections or attachments, such as budget reports, a Change Log, or an Issues Log. It's not easy to come up with the right combination of information that will be of interest to all readers. In fact, you may need a detailed status report for the stakeholders interested in your project as well as a higher-level summary status report for more senior managers interested in the project, but who don't have enough perspective and context to understand the details.

The bottom line is that project managers should take pride in their status reports and try to provide relevant and clear information to their readers. If your readers are not clear on how the project is progressing, you have not done an effective job.

Update Your Risk Plan Throughout the Project

Lauren Carter was a tall woman who had made a big name for herself locally playing basketball. She still ranked in the top ten for most career points in Illinois high school girls basketball history and was one of the state leaders for most rebounds. She played high school ball in Dickens for Thomas Jefferson High School before moving on to college ball at the University of Illinois. She graduated with a degree in business and played a little professional basketball. However, the women's side of the sport was not as popular back then as it is today, and she ended up using her business degree instead of her basketball skills in the workforce. She was a good project manager who had gained a lot of respect at Mega Manufacturing from her peers. She called me Wednesday morn-

ing and asked to meet me that same day. When I met with her, it was clear right away that a problem had developed.

Lauren was managing a project to make all the hard-copy reports supporting the factory floor available through the Web. The project was maybe two-thirds complete.

"Sounds like there's a problem with your project, Lauren. What's the latest?" I asked.

"Yes, we've got a big problem," she said, taking a deep breath. "We have been using the beta release of a web reporting tool and it has worked pretty well. However, the vendor announced this morning they have been purchased by one of their competitors. The vendor is no longer sure they will bring this reporting tool to market, since the company purchasing them has a very similar product. This has really thrown a monkey wrench into our plans, and it will certainly affect our project end dates. First, we will have to decide on a new tool and then retest everything. I want to talk to you about some ideas we have to resolve this. Each potential solution has some positives and negatives."

"I'm glad you at least have a couple options for resolving the tool problem," I said. "Didn't you have a chance to see this possible outcome occurring?"

"When we started the project, we looked at the risk of using this vendor," Lauren replied, shaking her head. "However, the risk seemed low at the time. They have a good product and they were financially sound. So, we made an assumption they were going to work out okay. We didn't see a need to include them in our risk management plan."

"Well, I'm sure that was the case when you started the project. But there has been some recent press about these two companies talking."

"Really?" Lauren leaned back, a little surprised. "I guess we haven't been keeping up on current events like we should."

LESSON

Risk management is one of the key project management processes performed in the initial project planning. The risk management process includes the following steps:

1. **Create a Risk Management Plan:** Start the risk management process by understanding your overall approach for managing risks. This includes defining your risk management process, who is involved with the risk management process, what tools will be used, etc.

2. **Identify all potential risks:** When you are defining the project, perform a complete assessment of project risk. The risk assessment is done in two parts. First, look at inherent risks. Inherent risks are based on the characteristics of the project—regardless of the specific deliverables being produced. Second, look for risks that are specific to your project. These risks normally can't be identified on a checklist since they are specific to your project and may not apply to other projects. At this point, you are not looking for only high-level risks—you are trying to identify **potential** risks.

3. **Analyze the risks using qualitative techniques:** In the prior step, you identified all potential risks. However, not all of the risks need to be managed. Now you analyze the risks to see which ones are important enough to manage. Qualitative analysis means that you use subjective criteria to decide which risks are high, medium, and low based on the probability of occurrence and the impact to your project.

4. **(Optional) Utilize quantitative analysis for all high-level risks:** If your project requires more rigor and a numerical understanding of the nature of risks, you can proceed to qualitative analysis. The term *quantitative* means that the risk levels are based on a numerical analysis rather than on approximations such as low, medium, and high.

5. **Create a response plan for each high-level risk:** Create a response plan for each high-level risk that you identified to ensure the risk is managed successfully. There are five major responses to a risk: leave it, monitor it, avoid it, move it to a third party, or mitigate it. You can also create a contingency plan for high-level risks that describes what you would do if the risk event actually occurs. (This is also called "Plan B.")

6.   **Move the activities associated with the risk response plans to the project schedule**: Moving the activities to the schedule helps ensure that the risk plan is actually completed.

Lauren and her team did a good job on the initial risk assessment. However, they did not do well on the remaining two follow-up activities.

1.   **Monitor the risk response plan:** Lauren needs to monitor the risk response plans to ensure they are being executed successfully. New activities should be added if it looks like the risk is not being managed successfully.

2.   **Periodically re-evaluate risks:** The initial risk management process needs to be repeated periodically throughout the project based on current circumstances. New risks may arise as the project is unfolding and some risks that were not identified earlier may become visible at a later date. This is also the time to validate the severity of known risk events. In addition, previously identified risk events may still be valid, but the likelihood or severity of the risk may have changed. This ongoing risk evaluation should be performed on a regular basis, say monthly, or at the completion of major milestones.

Lauren, like many other project managers, performed the initial risk assessment, but she did not perform the follow-up and ongoing risk management processes. Just as the schedule needs to be updated on an ongoing basis, so the risk plan needs to be double-checked throughout the project.

Lauren's team initially identified a risk with the software maker, but they felt the risk was low. Therefore, they assigned it to the level of an assumption. That was fine at first, but Lauren and her team did not go back and periodically update the risk plan. If they had re-evaluated the plan, they would have looked at this low-level vendor risk. There is a good likelihood they would have seen that the vendor was in acquisition talks. This knowledge would have allowed them to raise the risk level and focus energy on looking at alternatives and contingencies.

If Lauren had upgraded this potential event from an assumption to a risk, the team would have had some time to deal with the situation. Of course, it doesn't mean the acquisition was more or less likely to occur. However, they could have considered alternatives, such as beginning to test the software of the acquiring company or other software packages.

Now that the event has occurred, the situation is classified as an issue and issues management techniques are utilized. The team may identify the same options for resolution as if they had done a risk plan earlier. However, if they had utilized a risk plan, they would have had time to prepare a plan of attack in case the event occurred. At this point, all they can be is reactive, and any resolution will probably have an impact on the timing of the project.

Don't Deliver More Than the Client Requested

The weeks between Thanksgiving and Christmas are traditionally slow times of the year at Mega Manufacturing. Many people take vacation time at the end of the year, and even if they don't, I find most people are ready for the Christmas break about two weeks before it arrives. As such, they very rarely schedule any new projects to start during this time frame, and if a project is near completion, every effort is made to wrap it up before the holidays.

When I arrived at my office on Monday morning following the Thanksgiving break, I was surprised to find a voicemail message from Sally White. Sally and I had been e-mailing back and forth about her team's project to enhance one of our purchasing systems. When we spoke last, Sally was trying to implement some structured project management processes to ensure this effort didn't become any larger. I decided to swing by her office after grabbing a cup of coffee.

Sally was in her mid-30s and happily single. She had light brown hair and hazel eyes, and she was an avid reader. She had three bookcases in her office, and they all were full to the point of overflowing.

"You're going to be able to open that public library very soon," I said after walking into her office.

"I know, right? I ordered a third book case only three years ago. Now it looks like I'll need to order a fourth."

"Or you could just unload some of the books you have. Have you ever thought about purchasing a Kindle or an iPad? I have an iPad with iBooks if you'd like to give that a try."

"I actually have a Kindle already, and I do use that for reading, especially when I travel. I don't know, though. There's just something about a physical book. I don't think you can beat it."

I took a few minutes to peruse Sally's bookcases. They were mostly filled with business books, although she also had some American literature classics and even the complete Harry Potter series. Needless to say, she appeared to read everything.

"Tom, I have some good news today," Sally began as I sat down in front of her desk. "We were able to formally gain agreement on the business requirements for this work. I think the problems I e-mailed you about regarding change are all in the past."

"That's good news," I replied. "As I said in one of my replies, you can't manage scope effectively if you haven't defined the scope to begin with."

We talked some more about the requirements. Sally was able to gain agreement on a minimum set of requirements from the manufacturing client. During the discussions, however, Sally uncovered other features that the client wanted. These were not included in the project for the sake of getting the initial work completed and implemented.

"When does it look like you will be done?"

"We have some more good news on that front," Sally said excitedly. "We initially told the client it would take an additional six weeks to complete the work. But, when we got into the initial programming, we discovered some of the work was not nearly as complex as we first feared. We have about two weeks less work than we thought."

"Great news!" I agreed. "I'm sure your client will be happy to implement this work earlier."

"Well, that is one option," Sally countered. "However, remember we uncovered a number of additional features the client wanted but didn't include in this enhancement. Now that we have some extra time, we can include this additional work as well. I think the client will be very happy when they see the extra features we will be able to implement and still deliver within the deadline they have already agreed to."

"Has your client approved the extra features?" I asked.

Sally looked a little puzzled. "Well, we didn't ask them officially. We thought it would be a nice surprise if we delivered the extra features. We know they wanted them initially."

On the surface, this sounded great. But I knew from experience and training this was not the right way to go. Sally was about to get into a case of gold plating.

LESSON

During the project planning process the project team understands the nature of the project in terms of deliverables, budget, duration, risk, etc. This information is used to set common expectations between the project team and the sponsor. Setting expectations is one of the reasons we ask the sponsor and key stakeholders to approve the Project Charter and the business requirements. If the project manager can then deliver within those expectations, the project is typically considered a success. However, like Sally, you may also have heard it is good to under-promise and over-deliver. Let's look at what it means to under-promise, since there is a good way and a bad way to do this.

The project manager has some options when setting expectations using one of three scenarios—worst case, most likely, and best case. The worst-case option means you assume everything will go wrong. Work will take longer than you expect, issues will come up, potential risks will occur, etc. If you set expectations based on the worst-case scenario, you are not under-promising—you are sandbagging. This means you are purposely setting very low expectations you know you can exceed. Sandbagging is not good because you are not presenting accurate information to the sponsor and therefore the sponsor does not have the right information to make the best business decisions.

The best-case scenario is just the opposite. If you present the best case, you are assuming everything will go according to plan and everything will work great the first time. This is also not a good way to set expectations and for the same reason. The sponsor can't make the best business decisions if information is skewed. Of course, you are also much more likely to be unsuccessful in meeting your expectations and this will cause trouble all around.

You can see that the best course of action is to set expectations based on events that are most likely to occur. This includes most likely estimates of schedule and budget, most likely risks, most likely constraints, etc.

With that in mind, let's look back at Sally's desire to under-promise and over-deliver. She has set reasonable expectations and now is able to exceed those expectations. Will her sponsor be happy because Sally is able to deliver more than they have requested? Maybe, but maybe not. In fact, the client may even be very upset.

The term *gold plating* refers to delivering more than the client requested. It's wrong for two reasons. First, the primary focus of the project should be to make sure you deliver what the client wants, on time and within budget. By adding additional work, the risk increases that the project will actually miss its deadline and budget. If Sally misses her deadline date, for instance, no one will want to hear that the date was missed because Sally added additional work to the project that the client did not ask for. Adding extra work adds a level of unnecessary risk.

Second, if you can deliver more than the client expected, it's also true that you could have delivered exactly what the client expected—under budget and earlier. In other words, you had a choice: meet expectations while finishing early and under budget, or exceed expectations while finishing on budget and on schedule. The decision of which option to take is not for the project manager to decide. This is a sponsor decision. It may well be the case that the sponsor would rather finish early and under budget. But if you don't ask the sponsor, you won't know.

In this case, Sally is taking it upon herself to make a business decision on what is of most value to the client. There may be some good reasons why the additional features were not included in her initial project scope. They may, in fact, have had marginal value for the client. There may be more value in having the solution implemented two weeks earlier. The point is that this is a sponsor decision and not one the project manager should make.

The bottom line is you should meet your commitments. It may also be a good practice to under-promise and over-deliver. However, you should over-deliver on schedule and budget. After you set most-likely expectations, there is no reason you can't strive to finish under-budget and ahead of schedule. You can also over-deliver in your professionalism and level of service to your client. However, it should not include delivering more re-quirements than were asked for. If you can deliver earlier or for less cost, let the client make the decision on what to do with this good fortune.

Make One Person Responsible for Each Activity

Several people in my section of the office were taking vacation time in December, and I was amazed at how quiet the hallways and corridors were with fewer people around. I could actually hear the Christmas music coming from Leon Hart's office, and he worked about six doors down from me. I decided to visit some project managers in their offices in order to escape the noise.

My first opportunity to talk to someone came when I met with Marc Reynolds to discuss his project to build a customized time reporting application for all IT contractors. Marc was an older man, probably in his late 50s, and didn't ask for help on his projects. In fact, the only reason we were meeting was because his boss had called me and asked me to check in on him. Apparently, Marc's project had encountered some trouble about a month ago, but the team was able to solve it and get back on schedule — at least up until two weeks ago. Now they were falling behind again.

"We are getting over the hump," Marc said in response to my question about his project status. "But as we are getting to the end of the project, I'm asking the team to do quite a bit of multitasking. As a result, some team members are having difficulty completing their assignments on time."

"It's not uncommon to have a rash of work to complete at the end of the project," I agreed. "This is the time where discipline and time management skills are so valuable. Tell me more about why the work is falling behind. Does everyone know what's expected of them?"

"I sure hope so!" Marc exclaimed. "I've tried to make it simple by dividing the group into two sub teams. Each sub team is responsible for about half the remaining work."

"That sounds reasonable," I replied. "What does your team say about missing their deadlines now that the project is so close to completion?"

"That's one of the frustrating side effects of having two sub teams. I'm trying to give the teams maximum flexibility to complete their assigned work in whatever way makes the most sense. However, since I am assigning work to a team, I don't really know who to hold accountable when deadline dates are missed."

I was starting to see the problem. "Marc," I said, "you may have taken the team concept a little too far. Although the work is given to a team, you still need to assign someone to be responsible for each activity. When people are working on multiple activities at the same time, it is especially important to have someone accountable for each activity."

LESSON

On a perfect team, all members would understand what is expected of them, and the members would all hold themselves accountable for meeting the expectations. There are actually some teams like this. These mature teams are sometimes called *high-performing teams*. Typically, work is assigned to the team and the team figures out how to do it. No project manager or team leader is needed. However, it may take a long time to reach this high-performing state—and many teams never reach this level.

In the real world, almost all teams fall short of this idealistic goal. When normal teams are asked to suddenly take on some of the traits of a high performing team, they can struggle. Sometimes the struggle can lead them to a higher level of performance more quickly. In most cases, however, a team presented with this situation will descend into confusion and chaos.

People don't always understand what is expected of them when they are left to work without proper guidance. In many cases, they overemphasize certain activities to the detriment of others. If there are problems, no one steps up to deal with them. In the worst case, anarchy breaks out as people thrash around amongst various activities without the focus needed to complete any of them on time. One of the purposes of having a project manager is to provide that central focus for leading and managing people on the project. On many projects, the project manager is the only person who maintains enough overall perspective to make the right decisions on priorities and resource requirements.

Just as a project needs one project manager, so each activity needs one person responsible for completing the work on time. If only one person is assigned to the work, the responsibility naturally falls on that one person. When activities are assigned to multiple team members, one person still needs to be responsible for ensuring the work gets done. This one person is responsible for providing status, escalating issues, and ensuring the work is completed on time.

Marc has reorganized his project team into two sub teams that he feels reflects the two major components of remaining work. He has restructured the team in a creative attempt to complete the remaining work as efficiently as possible. He feels if each team focuses on one of the two remaining areas of work, they can complete the work much faster.

His idea may be a good one, but there is a problem. He has opened the door to a potential loss of focus by not assigning one person to be primarily responsible for the work of each team. Since each team has a number of activities assigned to it, team members are working on more than one thing. This multitasking has left a vacuum in terms of responsibility. When work is trending late, there is no one to prioritize the work to ensure it is completed as efficiently as possible. If problems arise, it's not clear who is responsible for resolving them. Each team member is assigned to other activities, so there is a tendency to work where there are no problems, and let the problem areas languish. This would not happen on a mature, high-performing team, but Marc's sub teams are not at that level yet.

Marc is not going to develop a high-performing team overnight. His short-term solution is to make sure every activity has a responsible person assigned to it. This doesn't have to be the same person. He can assign each of the members of a sub team to be responsible for specific activities. In this way, each activity has one person responsible for making sure that it is completed on time, escalating issues, providing status updates, and ensuring that work is progressing. This person has an interest in making sure the activity is completed successfully.

So it is with all activities. If multiple people are assigned to one activity, the project manager must be clear on who has the overall responsibility for completion.

Focus on Deadlines to Keep Your Project from Wandering

A week before the Christmas holiday, I paid a visit to Lauren Carter, the project manager responsible for moving the old shop floor batch reports to the Web. When I last met with her, she was only a couple weeks away from finishing the project. It had been six weeks, and she was still four weeks away from finishing. I liked going to her office because she had a large display of sports memorabilia including several basketballs from her high school days commemorating the records she had broken plus several autographed balls and jerseys. My favorite was a pair of sneakers autographed by Michael Jordan.

"What's going on, Lauren?" I asked.

"Come on in, Tom. Not much happening here, just trying to get this project finished."

"Have any grand plans for the holidays?"

"Not really, Tom. I'm going to visit my mom down in Florida, so that will be nice. Will be good to see the sun again and escape the cold for a few weeks. We'll just have a quiet Christmas, though. Nothing too exciting. How about you?"

"Sort of the same plan although we're staying here in Dickens. I'm surprising the family with a trip to Disney World, so that will be the big Christmas present from Santa under the tree. We're not leaving until next February, though."

"That's great, Tom! Very exciting!"

"So let's chat for a few minutes about your project. It seems to be going on much longer than you had anticipated, yet I don't see or hear any indication that you are behind schedule."

"There have been a number of changes requiring us to push the end date out," Lauren said. "However, you will be glad to know I am invoking change management. Our sponsor approves each change, so we have been getting extra funding and extensions on our deadline."

"That explains why no one is complaining," I noted. "What types of change requests are you receiving?"

"They are mostly for additional features and functions, and small changes to our current deliverables," Lauren said, yawning. "That's one reason why we have been able to accommodate most of them successfully. They don't require a lot of work from our team."

"What does the future look like?" I asked. "Are you going to be able to complete the project by the end of January?"

"It's not clear," Lauren replied a bit apprehensively. "Most of the shop floor supervisors don't have extensive web experience. Now that they are getting more familiar with the technology, they are finding more and more things they want to incorporate."

"That's not entirely good," I said with some concern. *"Projects are temporary endeavors to produce a set of deliverables. They need to end at some point. I'm afraid you may be in a position where your project goes on and on, with minor changes bringing only incremental and marginal business value."*

"You're right," Lauren agreed. *"In fact, I think the team is starting to lose focus and energy. I have some concerns that we are getting a little sloppy in our testing and may end up missing something."*

"Let's talk with your sponsor about bringing the project to a close," I suggested. *"This doesn't mean your clients can't make additional changes. If there is business value in additional modifications, let's consider them to be enhancements after the project goes live."*

LESSON

On most projects, the project sponsor and project team are focused on completing the original work within the agreed budget and deadline. If anything, the team usually struggles to get all the work done by the deadline. In fact, there are many times when the deadline date may slip a few days so that work is not too rushed, which could cause implementation problems. On most projects, completing within a few days of your deadline is still satisfactory.

If the project is important enough, you typically don't have time to wander too far past the deadline date. If you are at risk of missing your deadline, your manager and sponsor start to get nervous and put pressure on the team to complete the work. The team may start to work overtime or new people may be assigned.

However, there are also some projects that have no specific end date. They may have a target end date, but there is no business driver for the date. It is simply the date on the schedule when the project should be completed. If there is no business driver for the end date, the project deadline is more likely to slip. The deadline date may get pushed out when change requests get approved. At other times, the team may not be able to get the work done by the original end date and the deadline gets pushed out. These delays are just accepted because there is no business urgency.

If you have a project with no firm business driver for the end date, it's important for the project manager to maintain the sense of urgency to finish by the estimated end date. If the deadline date has to be extended, it's important for the project manager to refocus the team on the new date. Having a focused end date gives team members a sense of urgency and helps them understand the importance of completing their work on time so that the entire project can be completed on time.

A problem arises, however, when the deadline date changes repeatedly. This can be caused by teams missing their first target date and then missing their revised target date and so on in what seems to be a never-ending cycle of work. This is a very bad situation from the standpoint of team morale and credibility. This is why it's important to make sure your deadline dates represent your best and most likely estimates. If you miss one deadline date, you don't want to miss a second deadline date.

Another reason that deadline dates slip repeatedly is because the client organization is also unfocused. It may be hard for the project team to get client input, gather requirements, get questions answered, etc. This, in turn, will drive project delays. In many cases, the sponsor knows that this is a problem. The sponsor still wants the project completed, but he is flexible on when it happens.

Ongoing scope change requests can also be a problem. If there is no urgency to complete the project, the sponsor may haphazardly approve scope change requests to strive for a more perfect solution. Lauren's project is a great example of this. Her sponsor is lax and is approving major and minor change requests on an ongoing basis, even at the end of the project. This is not scope creep per se, since the project manager and sponsor are actively managing and approving the changes. However, her sponsor is also introducing risk. There is a growing risk that striving for the perfect solution will cause the team to get careless and unfocused, which could mean lower quality and more problems toward the end of the project.

At this point, the best approach for Lauren is to work with the sponsor to freeze all changes. This allows the team to focus on final testing and implementation. New requirements are still permitted, but the team will place them on a prioritized backlog list. This list will be reviewed after the application goes live and is stable. Changes will then be considered as enhancements. They can be worked on by the support organization or perhaps by planning a new phase II project. However, this first project needs to be wrapped up before the lack of focus leads to new problems.

Gain Agreement on Project Metrics Ahead of Time

My last meeting of the year was with Heather Cruise. Heather pulled me aside at the annual Christmas lunch to ask if I could attend a project conclusion meeting with her later that week.

Heather was assigned to a project for the Finance Division after the previous project manager resigned. The project was already experiencing some problems, which was probably a factor in the previous project manager leaving the country. It had been a tough spot for Heather, but she had done an admirable job in bringing the project to completion. The solution was finally implemented, but there was still some question as to whether the project was successful or not. I attended the project conclusion meeting, and I could tell it didn't go as Heather expected. She came prepared with a set of metrics to show that her team was somewhat successful on the project, but the business client didn't accept her metrics at face value. Afterward, we talked in her office.

"Heather, it appears there was a difference of opinion on whether the project was successful or not," I began. "I first wanted to compliment you. You attempted to initiate a fact-based discussion to show the state of the project. Why do you think it didn't work out the way you planned?"

"There was a lot of emotion built up over the course of the project," Heather replied in a serious tone, her eyes widening. "I came into the project late and didn't realize the level of dissatisfaction some of the clients felt with the previous project manager. Since there was so much emotion involved, I tried to bring the discussion around to some fact-based metrics."

"It sounded like the client was challenging the validity of some of your numbers and whether they were relevant," I noted. "For instance, you said the project completed on schedule, but the client said the solution was implemented without adequate testing."

"That may or may not be the case," Heather countered defensively, shaking her head back and forth. "We all agreed we would implement on the revised deadline date and fix any problems on an ongoing basis. Having agreed to that decision, I don't know how they can complain about the project being late."

"Yes, but the client said they were pushed into that decision because they could not afford to miss this monthly financial close cycle," I noted.

Heather was about to respond, but I realized the current line of reasoning wasn't going anywhere. Nor should it, since it wasn't the general lesson I was trying to teach.

"Heather, let me stop you for a minute. You have the right idea about the importance of project metrics. If you measure the right characteristics of your project, you will be in a much better position to improve your processes during the project and have a fact-based discussion about overall project success or failure. But your metrics seemed to be designed to show the project team in a more favorable light. You also missed a very important part of project success metrics—you must gain agreement with your client ahead of time."

LESSON

It has been said there are facts, lies, and then there are statistics. Statistics, or metrics, can be gathered on myriad combinations of project team and deliverable characteristics. For instance, you can collect metrics on the height of team members, the number of reporting errors, the daily high temperature in Dickens, and the cost of a project. Although there are dozens (or hundreds) of metrics you can gather, some of them are obviously more relevant and significant to the project than others.

One of the purposes of metrics is to objectively determine the level of project success. However, the project manager can't pick an arbitrary set of metrics to indicate success. It is the client, and specifically the sponsor, who ultimately determines project success. You could just ask the sponsor if the project was a success. However, gathering metrics gives you a more objective way to measure success rather than just relying on the perception (or the whim) of the sponsor.

One of the purposes of gaining agreement on the initial project charter is that it provides a set of deliverables upon which success or failure can be measured. The project manager should be aware of these when gathering metrics during the project. Delivering the agreed upon deliverables could be the starting point for a set of project success metrics.

Heather understood that metrics were important to try to show project success. She realized that without more facts, the client was going to conclude the project was a disaster. However, she failed to do two important things. First, she failed to get an agreement with the sponsor on the significance and the interpretation of the metrics she chose. Second, she didn't make sure the metrics were balanced and broad enough to represent the reality of the project experience. Since there was a disagreement on the metrics gathered and what they meant, Heather was challenged right away.

Heather's client was not happy with the way the project was run and was not happy with the system that was implemented. So, not surprisingly, they didn't agree with metrics saying the project was a success or a partial success. Heather's metrics seemed to be a narrow set attempting to show the results in as favorable a light as possible.

Heather would have been better off proposing a wider range of metrics to her client, including:

- Actual costs expended compared to the budget.
- Actual completion date compared to the original deadline.

- Quantitative metrics describing the solution's performance, including response time and defects.
- Qualitative metrics describing client satisfaction with the solution, including ease of use, look and feel, etc.
- Survey feedback describing the client's satisfaction with how the project team performed, including how quickly the team responded to problems, how well they communicated, how well they partnered, etc.

Heather should have made sure there was an agreement with the sponsor on the metrics to collect and how to interpret the results. Normally this is done at the beginning of the project. However, since Heather came to the project late, she should have gained agreement when she first came on board. Then her team could have focused on the proper success factors, and, when the project ended, she could have collected the metrics and had the fact-based discussion she was hoping for. A balanced set of project metrics would probably include client satisfaction, and since the client was not happy, the final results were still not going to indicate total success. However, a good set of metrics does give everyone the right facts with which to have a discussion about what went right and what could be improved. If you have an unapproved, arbitrary, and skewed set of metrics, you are not going to get anywhere in a discussion.

Year-End Recap

I have enjoyed my job over the past year, and I hope I was able to provide value to the project managers in our organization. The preceding stories represent only a fraction of the meetings and coaching sessions I participated in during the year. I tried to pick out stories that highlight some of the most valuable project management lessons. Of course, there are many others.

The year has not only been fun, but it has been professionally rewarding for two reasons. First, I have been able to see the project managers learn and grow. Some were already skilled in the project management discipline, but others had never before received formal training or coaching and didn't really know what it meant to manage a project—people like Jerry Ackerman.

Of course, the majority of the project managers were in between—people like Lindsay, Sean, and Ashley. They came from various organizations but all had some project management skills, even a little training. However, they managed projects via a sense for how to organize and manage the work, rather than by utilizing specific project management practices.

Second, my work this year has set the stage for the real project management deployment initiative that is scheduled to begin next year. Our company executives feel there is much more value to be gained by managing projects more efficiently and consistently.

The President's plan for establishing the initial Project Management Office (PMO) has been approved. The project is being funded as a three-year initiative, after which the PMO will move from deployment mode to long-term support of the project environment. It promises to be challenging—culture change always is. However, I hope the work I have done this year has set the stage for this broader initiative in the years ahead. If we are successful, a new project-driven culture will emerge, allowing all project managers to successfully deliver projects faster, with higher quality, and at less cost than we do today.

Wish us luck in this initiative! (Perhaps this initiative would make for a good book in the future.)

Index

M, N, O

Metrics, 49, 50, 139, 157, 215
  causes and impacts, 160
  client's perspective, 160
  collecting data, 141
    manual process, 142
    sponsor's opinion, 142
    time and cost, 141
  collecting metrics, 51
  defining and collecting, 51
  gathering metrics, 217
  help desk and IT support team, 159
  plant management, 159, 160
  proposing metrics to client, 217
  purposes
    gaining agreement, 217
    project success, 217
Milestones, 169, 171
  managers and sponsors,
    tracking, 171
  project management
    checkpoint, 171
  scheduling activities, 172

P

Performance feedback, 53
  project manager, 55, 56
  team members
    escalate to functional
      manager, 56
    gathering facts, 55
    giving immediate feedback, 55
    meet in person, 55–56
Postmortems. *See* End-of-Project
  Review Meeting
Prevention (QA), 88
Proactive project management
  process. *See* Risk management
Project characteristics
  common objectives, 6
  defined scope, 6
  deliverables, 6
  finite time frame, 5

management and leadership, 5
operations work, 5
overhead, 5
project manager and project
  team, 6
set of resources, 6
support work, 5
uniqueness, 6
Project charter, 43
Project deadline, 211
  client organization unfocused, 232
  date changes repeatedly, 232
  implementation problems, 231
  no firm business driver, 231
  scope change requests, 232
Project delivery, 209
  best-case scenario, 212
  commitments, 213
  gold plating, 212
  most likely expectation, 212
  sandbagging, 212
  setting expectations, 211
  worst-case option, 211
Project management, 7, 19
  cancel projects, 77
    business value, 79, 80
    investment, 80
    project failure, 79
  change management, 21
  client, 9
  enhancements, 21
  formal project management, 22
  Project Charter, 21
  risk management. *See* Risk
    management
  sponsors, 9
    active sponsor, 9
    executive/tactical project
      sponsor, 9
    issues and changes, 9
    transitioning, 10
Project planning, 101, 103
  project execution, 103
  project manager, 103

HD
69
. P75
M626
2011

CPSIA information can be obtained at www.ICGtesting.com
Printed in the USA
LVOW102131031011

248959LV00003B/5/P

9 781430 238348